Sheds

Sheds

The Do-It-Yourself Guide for Backyard Builders

Revised and Expanded

Written and Illustrated by
David Stiles

FIREFLY BOOKS

A FIREFLY BOOK

Second Edition 1998
Third Printing 2000

Cataloguing in Publication Data

Stiles, David R.
        Sheds: the do-it-yourself guide for backyard builders

Rev. & expanded.
Includes index.
ISBN 1-55209-292-5

1. Outbuildings – Design and construction –
Amateurs' manuals.
I. Title.

TH4955.S75   1998   690'.89   C98-931024-8

Published in Canada in 1998 by
Firefly Books Ltd.
3680 Victoria Park Avenue
Willowdale, Ontario M2H 3K1

Published in the United States in 1998 by
Firefly Books (U.S.) Inc.
P.O. Box 1338, Ellicott Station
Buffalo, New York 14205

We acknowledge the financial support of the Government of Canada through the Book Publishing Industry Development Program for our publishing activities.

Original design by Susan Spinelli
Illustrations by David Stiles
Photography by Skip Hine
Cover photograph by Skip Hine

Printed and bound in Canada by
Friesens
Altona, Manitoba

Printed on acid-free paper

Notice: The information contained in this book is true, complete and accurate to the best of our knowledge. All recommendations and suggestions are made without any guarantees on the part of the author or Firefly Books. The author and publisher disclaim all liability incurred in connection with the use of this information.

To my wife, Jeanie, who helped me in so many ways.

JEANIE STILES

About the Author

DAVID STILES IS A PROFESSIONAL DESIGNER, builder and architectural renderer whose clients include: I.M. Pei, Hartz Mountain, and Ford Motor Company. A graduate of the Pratt Institute and the Academy of Fine Arts in Florence, Italy, he is the author and illustrator of five how-to books, including *The Tree House Book,* a bestseller. His articles have appeared in *House Beautiful, Popular Mechanics, American Home* and the *New York Times.* He divides his time between Manhattan and East Hampton, New York.

Acknowledgments

I would like to thank Lionel Koffler and Michael Worek of Firefly Books for their avid enthusiasm and continuous support of *Sheds*.

Imperial to Metric Conversion Table

Measures of Length—Basic S.I. Unit—
Metre = 100 Centimetres = 39.37 Inches

Inches		1	2	3	4	5	6	7	8	9	10	11
Feet	Centi-meters	2.54	5.08	7.62	10.16	12.70	15.24	17.78	20.32	22.86	25.40	27.94
1	30.48	33.02	35.56	38.10	40.64	43.18	45.72	48.26	50.80	53.34	55.88	58.42
2	60.96	63.50	66.04	68.58	71.12	73.66	76.20	78.74	81.28	83.82	86.36	88.90
3	91.44	93.98	96.52	99.06	101.60	104.14	106.68	109.22	111.76	114.30	116.84	119.38
4	121.92	124.46	127.00	129.54	132.08	134.62	137.16	139.70	142.24	144.78	147.32	149.86
5	152.40	154.94	157.48	160.02	162.56	165.10	167.64	170.18	172.72	175.26	177.80	180.34
6	182.88	185.42	187.96	190.50	193.04	195.58	198.12	200.66	203.20	205.74	208.28	210.82
7	213.36	215.90	218.44	220.98	223.52	226.06	228.60	231.14	233.68	236.22	238.76	241.30
8	243.84	246.38	248.92	251.46	254.00	256.54	259.08	261.62	264.16	266.70	269.24	271.78
9	274.32	276.86	279.40	281.94	284.48	287.02	289.56	292.10	294.64	297.18	299.72	302.26
10	304.80	307.34	309.88	312.42	314.96	317.50	320.04	322.58	325.12	327.66	330.20	332.74
11	335.28	337.82	340.36	342.90	345.44	347.98	350.52	353.06	355.60	358.14	360.68	363.22
12	365.76	368.30	370.84	373.38	375.92	378.46	381.00	383.54	386.08	388.62	391.16	393.70
13	396.24	398.78	401.32	403.86	406.40	408.94	411.48	414.02	416.56	419.10	421.64	424.18
14	426.72	429.26	431.80	434.34	436.88	439.42	441.96	444.50	447.04	449.58	452.12	454.66
15	457.20	459.74	462.28	464.82	467.36	469.90	472.44	474.98	477.52	480.06	482.60	485.14
16	487.68	490.22	492.76	495.30	498.84	500.38	502.92	505.46	508.00	510.54	513.08	515.62
17	518.16	520.70	523.24	525.78	528.32	530.86	533.40	535.94	538.48	541.02	543.56	546.10
18	548.64	551.18	553.72	556.26	558.80	561.34	563.88	566.42	568.96	571.50	574.04	576.58
19	579.12	581.66	584.20	586.74	589.28	591.82	594.36	596.90	599.44	601.98	605.52	607.06
20	609.60	612.14	614.68	617.22	619.76	622.30	624.84	627.38	629.92	632.46	635.50	637.54

Example:
(1) To convert 13 feet 6 inches to centimetres, read along line 13 under feet and under column 6 inches read 411.48 cms. To reduce to metres move decimal point two spaces to left; thus, 4.1148 metres is the answer.

Fractional Equivalents

in.–cms.	in.–cms.
1/16 = 0.15875	1/8 = 0.31700
3/16 = 0.47625	1/4 = 0.63500
5/16 = 0.79375	3/8 = 0.95250
7/16 = 1.11125	1/2 = 1.27040
9/16 = 1.42875	5/8 = 1.58730
11/16 = 1.74625	3/4 = 1.90500
13/16 = 2.06375	7/8 = 2.22250
15/16 = 2.38125	1 = 2.54000

Contents

Shed interior

Introduction

❧

I have had a passion for building small structures since I was a kid. My first project, a clubhouse, ended in total failure because I did not know how to plan joints. Since then, I have built numerous treehouses, huts and forts. Now I have graduated to building sheds. Sheds, after all, are simply small houses, and many of the same principles apply to building both. If you plan on building your own house, you should definitely start by building a shed. This will not only test your building skills, but it will also give you a place to put your tools so they won't rust or get stolen. Even if you don't have such lofty home-building goals, a shed tailored to your needs and built by you and perhaps family and friends is a long-lasting, satisfying structure.

Let me dispel some common myths right away. Don't be misled by your neighbor saying, "You can build a shed in a weekend." All sheds take longer to build than you may think. To build anything right means you have to build it carefully; that takes time. How much time depends on your skills and the complexity of the shed you choose to build. A safe rule of thumb is to figure out the time required for each step and double it.

Another myth is that if you build the shed yourself, it won't cost anything. Not true. Even a doghouse will cost something in materials. Lumber is not cheap. You may be thinking of scavenging used lumber—be aware that using old lumber of different sizes and strengths can lead to problems later on and may add unnecessary building time.

The shed you build yourself can be built better than any you may buy. You can build it to last a lifetime, you can build it to meet your exact requirements, you can build something you will be proud of. You can build a shed that will make you feel good every time you open the door and smell that unforgettable scent of real wood and see the shed that you put together with your own hands.

A recent study explored the success of home centers across the United States. The tool and hardware departments were getting a lot of business from "weekend carpenters." Most were business people who spent a large part of their lives in offices. The study found that what most of these people lacked in their lives was being able to have total control over a project and to feel the satisfaction that resulted from beginning the project and carrying it to completion themselves. Building a shed provides you with just that.

Building a shed is a big project and an activity that you should take pleasure in doing. In order to avoid mistakes and the frustration of trying to meet a deadline, allow plenty of time for completion. Make it an open-ended project that you can enjoy.

Any homeowner, especially those without a garage or basement, will be amazed what a difference a shed makes to their property. Not enough room for storage is one of homeowners' top complaints, according to the National Association of Home Builders.

Once you have completed a shed, you may find that your awareness of sheds has been elevated. As you drive through the countryside, your eye will unavoidably be drawn to people's yards, and you may quite naturally begin appraising the success or failure of other sheds. You may even feel inclined toward replacing that silver-framed photo of your trusting family dog with a color photo of your shed!

Sheds is different from the few other existing shed books or shed chapters in more general books, because it helps you get started thinking through what you want in your shed and then helps you design a shed to fit your needs. I begin with a compendium of construction techniques—it helps to get familiar with these at the design stage and to refer to them again during actual building. The book continues with simple step-by-step, illustrated instructions for building a basic 8 x 10 shed from the bottom up. A section on a few more basic sheds is followed by a sampling of more complex special-use sheds whose designs come from hand-crafted outbuildings all over the world. I have included plans for all the sheds described in the book. I have purposely chosen designs with very different construction techniques and architectural features so that you can actually combine elements from various designs to create your custom-made shed. Perhaps you want to include the pole framing of the Japanese Boat Shed in your work shed along with the window of the Basic 8 x 10 Shed. The possibilities are endless. Finally, for the confident craftsperson and the dreamer there is a section of inspirational drawings and color photographs—ideas to incorporate and ideas to build on.

Sheds is written for creative, hands-on homeowners with do-it-yourself experience in weekend projects and basic home repair. You should have at least a few building and repair projects under your tool belt, be ready to tackle medium-sized, challenging projects and be willing to stretch your carpentry skills for worthwhile accomplishments.

CHAPTER 1

Designing Your Shed

❧

Building Permit

Before deciding to build a shed, call your local building
inspector to determine whether you need a building permit
or whether you will be allowed to build a shed at all.
Requirements vary among localities. In many rural communities,
sheds are considered accessory buildings, and it is not necessary to file
for a building permit. Other communities allow any structure under 120
square feet to be built without a permit—you could build a generous-
sized 10 x 12 shed. Still other areas will allow any 36-square-foot structure without a permit. Some building inspectors allow you to build a
"temporary" shed as long as it is not permanently attached to the
ground and could be moved at a future date. Still others require both a
survey to indicate where the shed will be placed and an "as-built" survey
upon its completion. This is done to aid the tax assessment of your
property each year. The survey also helps establish the distance the shed
must be from the property line—called "setback." In most communities
this is determined by the zoning department or board and enforced by
the building inspector. Most zoning laws, for instance, will not allow a
shed in the front yard. Others limit a structure's height and the percent-
age of the lot that it occupies. Many zoning regulations allow an "accessory building" to be placed closer to the property line than a primary
structure. And they may restrict the use that an accessory building can
serve, for instance, not allowing "habitual living" or "quartering of live
animals."

You may also be required to submit plans to your homeowners' association or historical preservation society for approval. As long as the shed you plan to build is not out of keeping with the architecture in your area, there should be no problem. As a venerable zoning board member in my community, a master carpenter himself, said, "a good shed is a joy to behold."

Once you know the regulations, go ahead and design your shed within the codes. Then submit your plans to the local board, fill out their standard forms, and within a few weeks, you'll have the permit to display at your building site. Only then should you begin construction.

Getting Ideas Onto Paper

Your notion of a shed may have begun as a mere wistful longing for some sturdy little building that will make life easier, more organized, more creative, more charming. Sheds are often built to create space for activities that might otherwise find a room in the house, such as woodworking, plant tending, arts and crafts, etc. When you compare the cost of an addition onto your house (averaging $20,000), a shed is a viable alternative.

Imagine your shed; does it match your house, or is it a total architectural departure that becomes a focal point on your property? Do you picture something traditional or contemporary? Functional or folly? Whether it's a toolshed, workshop, potting shed or playhouse that you imagine, start a list of what it will be used for and an inventory of what will go inside. If it is a toolshed, a helpful reality check is to measure the tiller, riding lawnmower, trailer, etc. that you expect to cram into an 8 x 12-footer. Thought should be given on how to remove one piece without disturbing the others. Visualize how tools hang on the walls and what you will store on the shelves. Consider a dual-function shed, partitioned into tool shop and playhouse, or some other combination.

Here are some questions to ask yourself:

What will the shed be used for?
How much storage space will it have?
Should I allow for future expansion?
Will I have to buy more tools?
How much will it cost?
How difficult will it be to build?
Will I have time to build it?
Will I enjoy building it?
Will the rest of the family like it?
Will my neighbors like it?

Think about your shed's proportions. Sheds look best if they are not too long and not too square. As a general rule, try for a 3 to 4 ratio (see Figure 1.1). For instance, a 12-foot-wide shed might look best if it is 16 feet long. Of course, a shed with a specific function (such as the Japanese Boat Shed on page 95) might be an exception to this rule.

Try to keep the width of the shed as seen from the shortest side (a)

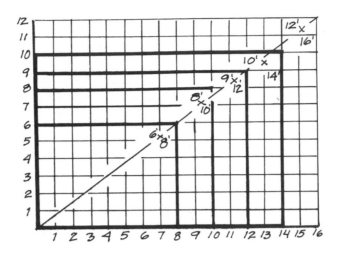

Figure 1.1—Typical shed sizes at 3 to 4 ratio

wider than the height of the eaves (b) (see Figure 1.2). This also helps makes the shed sturdier and more wind resistant.

Door height and slope are important factors in determining the size of your shed. Both are covered in detail in Chapter 2.

Next, look at possible sites on your property. Keep in mind your community's zoning setback regulations, the levelness of the ground, drainage, overhanging trees, orientation to sun and the shed's relation to other buildings. Picture your shed site in all seasons. Remember that when the leaves fall, people will be able to see more of your yard, including your shed. Choosing a shed that complements your house, and placing it where it relates well to other elements in your landscape is a lasting decision.

Then with decisions made on the basics, study the designs in this book, there's probably one that fits your needs. If there is, you are all ready to go ahead and build one of those right from the plans. If you'd like to combine designs or develop your own complete plans, dive in.

If you haven't already, begin making rough sketches of your shed—drawings, floor plans, elevations, whatever helps you see what will be. Mark or list approximate measurements as you go. Photograph the site from various angles. Buy a piece of tracing paper or prepared acetate from your art-supply store. Lay the paper or acetate over the photographs, and sketch the shed. By referring to the objects in the photo that you know the height of, you should be able to plot fairly accurately where the shed should be built and how it will look.

The combination of your inventories of needs and the size of the site

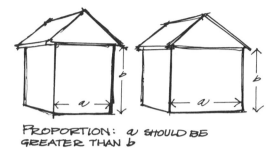

PROPORTION: *a* SHOULD BE
GREATER THAN *b*

Figure 1.2—Shed proportions

determine the shed size. You can fine-tune the size and eliminate a lot of
scrap by being aware of standard building material sizes. Lumber, for
example, usually begins at 8 feet in length and increases in 2-foot increments. Both studs and exterior sheathing and paneling products, such as
plywood, come most commonly in 8-foot lengths. For width, walls divisi-
ble into 4-foot increments are perhaps the most efficient to build, because
they match both multiples of framing intervals (16 or 24 inches for walls,
24 inches for rafters or trusses) and widths of paneling products such as
plywood (commonly 4 feet wide). The shed's use should, of course, be the
primary consideration when planning size, but it can sometimes be worth
rounding up or down a few inches to save cutting and lumber.

And lastly, set a budget goal for the shed so that later when you figure
out exactly what you want and what it will cost, you can see where you
can upgrade or cut back on the plans.

Drafting and Evaluating the Design

Now that you have decided what your specific needs are, it's time to
make a working plan.

From the sketches and approximate measurements that you have
accumulated, draw your plans on ¼-inch-square grid paper. If your shed
is more than 20 feet long, allow 1 square to equal 1 foot. If your shed is
20 feet or less, allow 2 squares—that is, ½ inch—to equal 1 foot (4
squares equals 1 square foot).

On separate pieces of paper, draw the floor plan, elevations of each
side, and cutaway (or section) views. There are many good introductory
books on architectural drawing if you need a hand.

From these plans you can generate a materials list and make some
phone calls to the lumberyard and hardware stores for prices and information on availability. If you find that the sizes of materials don't jibe
with your original thoughts or what you want is not in stock and you do
not want to wait, now is the no-cost time to adapt the plans. Add all
your estimated costs, and if the bottom line is some distance from your
original goal, go back to the drawing board.

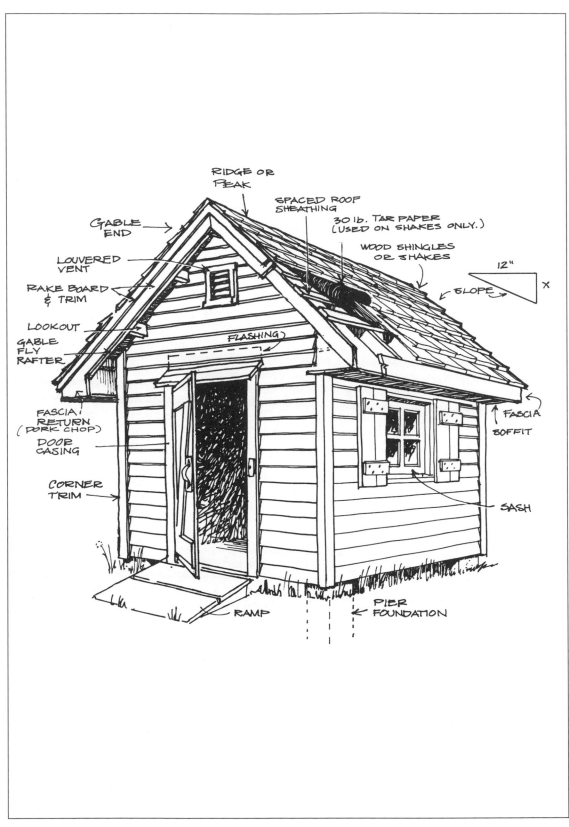

RIDGE OR PEAK

SPACED ROOF SHEATHING

30 lb. TAR PAPER (USED ON SHAKES ONLY.)

WOOD SHINGLES OR SHAKES

12"

SLOPE

X

GABLE END

LOUVERED VENT

RAKE BOARD & TRIM

LOOKOUT

GABLE FLY RAFTER

FLASHING

FASCIA RETURN (PORK CHOP)

DOOR CASING

CORNER TRIM

FASCIA

SOFFIT

SASH

RAMP

PIER FOUNDATION

Figure 2.1—Shed terms

CHAPTER 2

General Shed Construction Primer

M any of the choices that determine shed design and building procedures are rooted in construction techniques. It is helpful to study the shed terms (Figure 2.1), construction details and step-by-step instructions several times: first, when you are getting a feel for what you want in a shed; second, throughout the design process; and once again when you are in the throes of the hands-on, hammer-and-nail work. This section presents shed features from the ground up.

As you read and use this book, keep in mind that specific situations and dimensions may vary for different builders. The dimensions and angles given in the book are to the best of our knowledge correct. During construction, however, dimensions may change when wood swells or contracts, depending upon climate and type of lumber. We recommend that you measure and remeasure during the course of construction and make any necessary adjustments before cutting lumber. We have tried to give you basic guidelines to help you understand the designs and, if necessary, adapt them to your various site conditions and limitations.

Materials

Lumber comes in many lengths, but is usually sold in 2-foot increments, starting with 8 feet. It is either sold in board feet (12 x 12 x 1 inches) or linear (running) feet. The price varies according to regional availability and the wood species. Ruling out the most expensive tropical hardwoods, the most decay-resistant are cypress, locust, redwood and cedar. It pays to check with knowledgeable people at local lumberyards and mills to see which weather-resistant locally grown species might work. In any case, #2 construction pine is most economical, and if you are lucky enough to live near a sawmill, you might be able to buy rough cut (green) unseasoned lumber that is perfect for shed construction. Another economical choice available in the northeast is #2 northern pine.

Whether you buy seasoned (kiln dried) wood or unseasoned (green) lumber, consider what joinery you'll use. If square-edged lumber is butt-jointed, you may not be happy with the slight gaps that may show

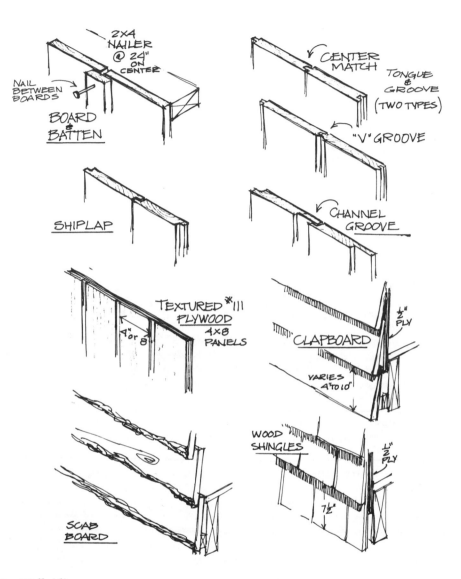

2X4 NAILER @ 24" ON CENTER

NAIL BETWEEN BOARDS

BOARD & BATTEN

CENTER MATCH

TONGUE & GROOVE (TWO TYPES)

"V" GROOVE

SHIPLAP

CHANNEL GROOVE

TEXTURED #III PLYWOOD 4X8 PANELS

4" or 8"

CLAPBOARD

½" PLY

VARIES 4" TO 10"

SCAB BOARD

WOOD SHINGLES

½" PLY

7½"

Figure 2.2—Wall siding

through on the inside when green lumber dries and contracts. Light filtering through a small crack makes the gaps appear much larger than they really are. One way to get around this is to nail a batten over the joint. Another solution is to use tongue-and-groove (referred to in some figures as T&G) or shiplapped lumber, which helps keep out weather and light and strengthens the shed considerably. Other joinery includes center match, "V" groove and channel groove. These wall siding options and others are shown in Figure 2.2.

Another alternative is to run boards horizontally. This is particularly advantageous if you are framing the shed using 2 x 4 studs vertically every 2 feet. If you are timber framing, you will have to add vertical

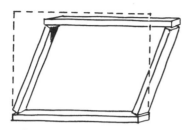

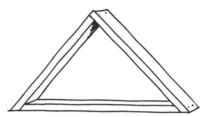

RACKED
RECTANGULAR FRAME

RIGID TRIANGULAR FRAME

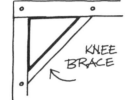

KNEE
BRACE

Figure 2.3—Triangulation

studs as nailers. Two types of horizontal siding make very attractive sheds. The first is the scab lumber sheathing—leftovers from the lumber mill. Second is clapboard; since it is only ½ inch thick, it should be nailed onto a ½-inch plywood base, and it requires trim at the corners and around the windows and doors. Other siding options include wood shingles and textured plywood.

Plywood—before its invention, framers built in diagonal braces to prevent the frame from getting "out of square." This is referred to as "triangulation" and is still used in all types of construction to stiffen a structure. Imagine, for instance, a rectangular frame. It can easily be bent out of shape. By removing one leg of the rectangle and joining the remaining corners, you are left with a triangle, which cannot be bent out of shape (see Figure 2.3).

Plywood is weak when used as a plank, but it is structurally strong when used as a skin nailed to a frame and when used on edge. The building industry is now making structural beams, gluing together many layers of plywood (called "glulams"), that rival steel girders in strength.

The obvious disadvantage of plywood is that the wood grain is not as aesthetically pleasing as natural planks. To improve its appearance, give plywood a coat of solid stain. The knotholes of economical grades, such as CDX exterior sheathing, may be filled with vinyl spackling compound (or, better yet, epoxy auto-body filler) before staining.

Timber Framing

Timber framing, sometimes referred to as post-and-beam construction, was the most common method of house construction up until the 20th century. Large timbers were joined together using mortise and tenon joints and wood pegs. With the advent of cheap nails and what appeared to be an endless supply of lumber, house builders in the United States switched to lightweight stick-built construction in the late 1800s. In recent years, however, there has been renewed interest in timber framing. Besides the aesthetic appeal of visible beams, timber framing offers other advantages—fewer cuts are necessary, and window and door headers can be eliminated.

One has only to visit an old barn to appreciate the skill and ingenuity that the Old World craftsmen used in joining the beams and posts together without nails. Remarkable craftsmanship is displayed in features of timber framing such as the tying joint (see Figure 2.3A), which joins several pieces of wood together at one point, and the scarf joint (see Figure 2.3B), which was used extensively in England when long pieces of lumber became scarce and smaller pieces were joined end to end to make up the required length. The most typical joint used in old barns is, of course, the ubiquitous mortise and tenon (see Figure 2.3C), which housewrights took great pride in crafting.

A simple method of building timber-frame sheds is to use lap joints (see Figure 2.3D and page 87 in the chapter on the Irish Garden Shed), which require only about five minutes to make. Used in combination with diagonal knee braces, this type of construction will produce a strong frame of which you can be proud.

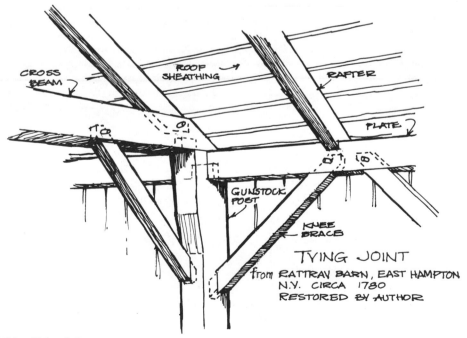

Figure 2.3A—Tying joint

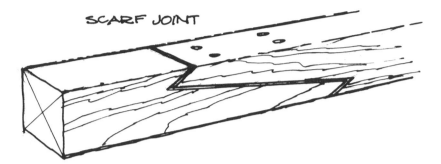

Figure 2.3B—Scarf joint

Figure 2.3C—Mortise and tenon joint

Figure 2.3D—Half lap joint

Setting the Offset Stakes

Construction of most sheds begins with marking the site with the exact shed measurements and making sure it is square. After you've chosen and prepared your site, visually line up one side of what will be the shed with the closest physical feature it relates to on your property, such as a fence, line of shrubs, driveway, road or house, and stake out two points parallel to this feature. Measure the distance with a tape or string, and make sure it is parallel (see Figure 2.4). Often the placement of the shed will be determined by the community's zoning setbacks.

Choose one side of the shed as a constant, and hammer two stakes into the ground deep enough so that they won't move, one at each end of this measurement. Drive a small nail in the top center of each stake. The easiest way to achieve a perfect rectangle is to create equal-length diagonals. Using a calculator, determine the lengths of the diagonals by using the simple formula that you learned in geometry class: $a^2+b^2=c^2$. For a 12 x 16 shed, for instance, applying the formula $a^2+b^2=c^2$, 12^2 (or 12 multiplied by itself) equals 144. Do the same for the "b" dimension, 16^2, or 16 x 16=256. Add these two numbers together (144+256) to get 400. To find the length of the diagonal, represented by "c," find the square root of c^2 (in this case, 400) by pressing the square-root button on your calculator and—presto—your diagonals are 20 feet each.

Place one tape measure on each of the corner stakes, 16 feet apart. The third corner will be where the diagonal (20 feet) and the 12-foot side intersect. Do the same to find the fourth corner. This will automatically create perpendicular corners (see Figure 2.5).

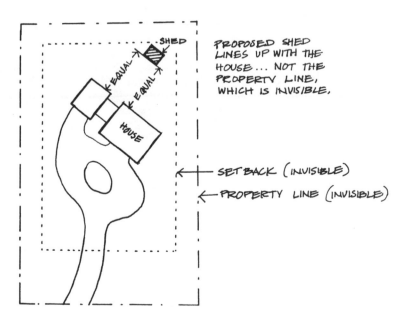

Figure 2.4—Placement

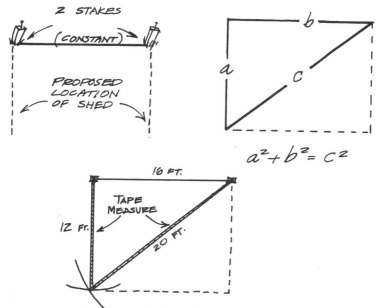

Figure 2.5—Creating perpendicular sides

The corner stakes will have to be removed if foundation postholes are dug; therefore, by placing "offset stakes," the corners of the shed can be relocated. Stretch a string around each pair of offset stakes to indicate perimeter of shed (see Figure 2.6). Remember, these cross lines represent the outside edge of your shed. Also, make sure the strings are level by raising or lowering them on the stakes (see Figure 2.7).

Foundations and Footings

A shed, no matter what its purpose or size, should be supported with a solid base. The type of foundation you choose depends on how permanent you want the shed. Most sheds are not permanently attached to the ground in order to be classified as a temporary structure and so they can be moved, if necessary.

A simple temporary foundation, like that of the classic 8 x 10 shed, requires a few concrete half blocks or flat rocks at the corners as described on page 53. The only risk is that in northern regions the shed might get out of level as a result of frost heaves. The movement will probably be slight and may correct itself by spring thaw. If your shed remains off-level, jack it up, using a hydraulic house jack, raise the shed to level and slip a slat shim under it (see Figure 2.8).

If you are building a permanent foundation, plan on spending a lot more time and money. Four types of foundation are stone masonry, concrete block, poured concrete slab and post-and-skirt.

Many people are attracted to stone foundations and, having seen them used in handsome old country sheds, would like to repeat stone's

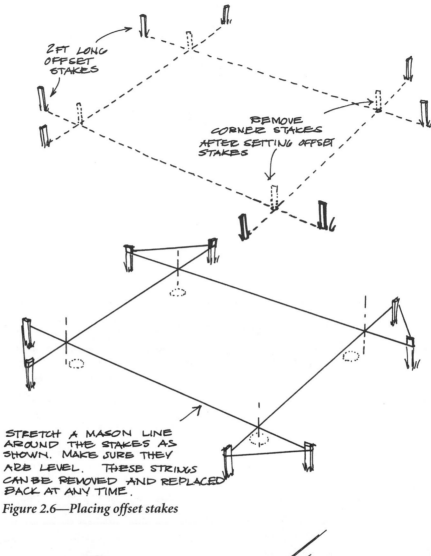

2FT LONG OFFSET STAKES

REMOVE CORNER STAKES AFTER SETTING OFFSET STAKES

STRETCH A MASON LINE AROUND THE STAKES AS SHOWN. MAKE SURE THEY ARE LEVEL. THESE STRINGS CAN BE REMOVED AND REPLACED BACK AT ANY TIME.

Figure 2.6—Placing offset stakes

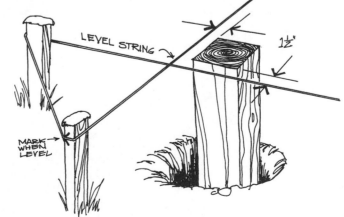

LEVEL STRING

$1\frac{1}{2}$"

MARK WHEN LEVEL

Figure 2.7—Allowance for framing

rustic appearance in their new sheds. If your property naturally turns up a lot of stone, a shed foundation is a great way to put it to good use. Placing stones under the sills (with or without mortar) will add to the attractiveness of the shed and keep out animals such as opossums and raccoons (see Figure 2.8A).

A more permanent foundation can be made using concrete blocks. Dig an 18-inch-wide trench to a depth below the frost line, and pour a footing 16 inches wide and 8 inches high on which you will lay the concrete-block wall. One advantage of a concrete-block foundation is that the blocks can be wheelbarrowed to sites that are difficult or impossible to reach with heavy equipment. Using a wheelbarrow also means that your lawn won't be destroyed by truck-tire ruts.

If, however, your site is easily accessible by tall, heavy ready-mix-concrete trucks, a poured concrete slab with a thickened edge (sometimes referred to as an Alaskan slab) is another alternative. Two advantages of a slab foundation are that you can pour the footing and the finished

Figure 2.8—Leveling a temporary foundation

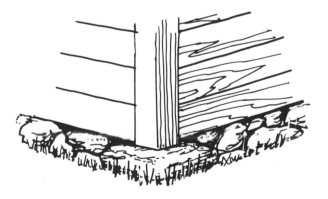

Figure 2.8A—Stone foundation

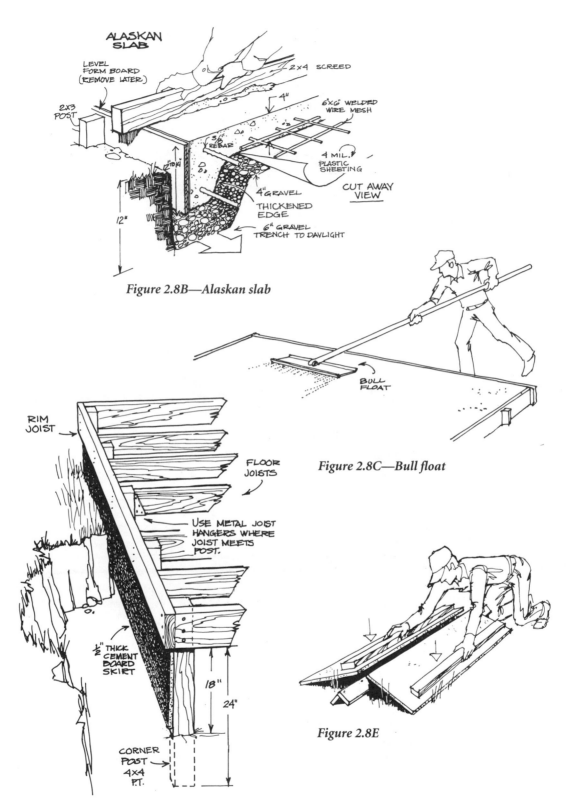

ALASKAN
SLAB

LEVEL
FORM BOARD
(REMOVE LATER)

2×4 SCREED

2×3
POST

4"

6"×6" WELDED
WIRE MESH

³⁄₈"
REBAR

4 MIL.
PLASTIC
SHEETING

4" GRAVEL

CUT AWAY
VIEW

12"

THICKENED
EDGE

6" GRAVEL
TRENCH TO DAYLIGHT

Figure 2.8B—Alaskan slab

Figure 2.8C—Bull float

BULL
FLOAT

RIM
JOIST

FLOOR
JOISTS

USE METAL JOIST
HANGERS WHERE
JOIST MEETS
POST.

½" THICK
CEMENT
BOARD
SKIRT

18"

24"

CORNER
POST
4×4
P.T.

Figure 2.8E

Figure 2.8D—Post-and-skirt foundation

floor at the same time and that little lumber is required for the forms. To support the slab, dig out the soil at the shed site to a depth of 4 inches, and fill it with gravel. Next, dig a 12-inch-deep trench around the perimeter of the shed footprint and fill it with 6 inches of gravel before pouring the concrete. Slope the trench downhill, and fill it with rocks, allowing any water that accumulates under the slab to drain out. Before pouring the concrete, lay down a sheet of 4-mil plastic and 6 x 6-inch welded wire mesh. As you pour the concrete, embed 1-inch rebar in the thickened edge (see Figure 2.8B).

If you have a strong back and your project requires only 1 or 2 cubic yards of concrete, you can mix it yourself in a rented mechanical concrete mixer. Use Type #1 95-lb. bags of cement, ž- to 1ž-inch-diameter crushed stone and clean sand delivered to your site. Mix them together in a ratio of one part cement, two parts sand, three parts gravel. Add as little water as possible for maximum strength—approximately 5 to 7 gallons of water per bag of cement. One bag of cement will yield almost 4 cubic feet of concrete. Before beginning, set up level form boards around the perimeter of your foundation. When you pour the concrete, use an extra-long 2 x 4 to "screed" off the concrete to make it level on top (see Figure 2.8B). Smooth the surface after it becomes dull-looking, using a trowel or a bull float (see Figure 2.8C). When you are finished, cover the slab with plastic sheeting to prevent it from drying too quickly, and wait several days for it to cure. Concrete reaches its maximum strength in 28 days.

A good alternative to a masonry foundation is a post-and-skirt foundation, which is easier to construct than a masonry foundation but just as efficient (see Figure 2.8D). After laying out the four corners with offset stakes and string (see pages 15-16), dig 24-inch-deep holes spaced 48

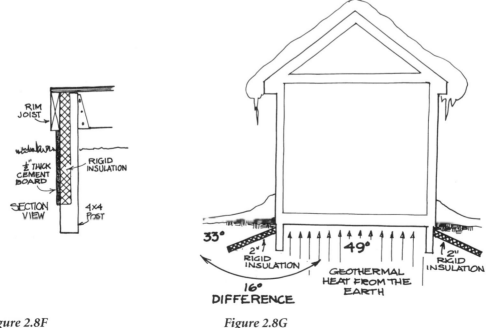

Figure 2.8F

Figure 2.8G

inches on center to hold 4 x 4 pressure-treated posts (see Glossary for precautions to take with pressure-treated lumber). Pressure-treated posts should be labeled "for ground contact." Temporarily attach the rim joists to the four corner posts. After checking to make sure that the posts and the frame are lined up square and level, attach the posts permanently using 2½-inch galvanized screws. Dig a narrow trench, and screw ½-inch-thick cement board to the posts. This will keep your floor warmer in the winter and help prevent animals from making a home under your shed. Cut each sheet of cement board in half lengthwise by scoring the fiberglass mesh with a utility knife and snapping it in half over a sharp edge (see Figure 2.8E). Nail the cement board to the posts. For a neat appearance, stucco the joints and corners with mortar. The

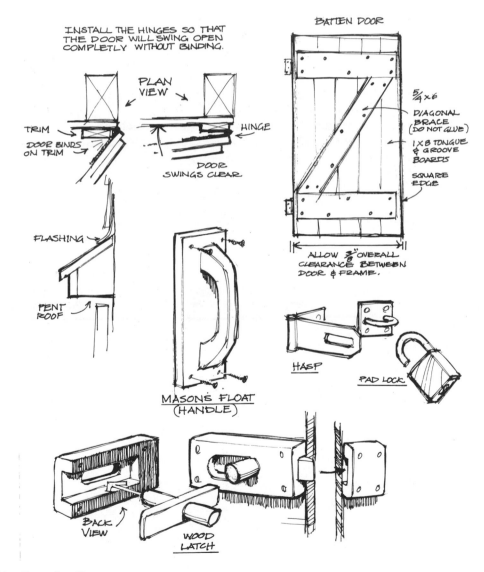

Figure 2.11—Door details

skirt can also serve as a surface to which rigid insulation can be attached if you plan to heat the shed. Backfill the trench so that the bottoms of the cement boards are buried in the ground.

If you plan to heat your shed in the winter and use it as an extra room such as a studio, insulate the foundation as well as the ceiling and walls. Do this by cementing 2-inch rigid insulation to the inside surface of the cement boards (see Figure 2.8F).

A relatively new innovation in this country, although it has been used for years in Scandinavia, is the frost-protected shallow foundation. By burying a skirt of 2-inch rigid insulation around the perimeter of the foundation, you can capture the geothermal heat that remains constant in the earth. It will protect the footings from frost heave, can raise the temperature of the floor by as much as 16 degrees F and will divert rainwater away from the foundation, keeping the space under the floor dry (see Figure 2.8G).

Doors and Door Height

Most shed doors are made from single, thick, 1 x 6 or 1 x 8 tongue-and-groove or shiplapped vertical boards with ⁵⁄₄ x 8 battens screwed to the back side. Doors can also be made of ¾-inch plywood and reinforced with battens. If the door is not protected by overhanging eaves, it

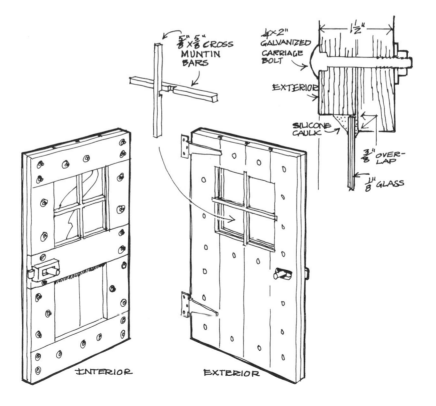

Figure 2.12—Double-thick tongue-and-groove door

should have a drip cap or small pent roof to keep out the weather (see Figure 2.11).

Handles can be of all sorts of types and sizes. An inexpensive handle can be made from a mason's wood float, sold in most supply stores (see Figure 2.11). Those with the necessary skills can make a wooden slide bolt that can be opened from either side of the door (see Figure 2.11); otherwise, the hardware store carries them at a reasonable price.

A more substantial 1½-inch-thick door can be made with double-thick tongue-and-groove cedar. (See Figure 2.12) Assemble enough tongue-and-groove boards to accommodate the width of your door opening. Cut out window opening with an electric jigsaw (saber saw). Bolt cross boards to the back with ¼x2-inch carriage bolts, overlapping the window opening by ⅜ inch. Cut a piece of ⅛-inch window glass to loosely fit the opening and install it in a bed of clear silicone caulk. For a more traditional look, add a cross muntin to the window, by mortising and notching two strips of ⅝x⅝-inch wood. Add the latch of your choice.

One more way to close the door on your project is to check the lumberyard for seconds, or doors ordered, but not picked up. The savings can be worthwhile. Purchase the door before you frame the opening so you can frame to fit.

Door height should be a minimum of 5 feet, 6 inches. This means many people will have to duck their heads slightly when entering the shed; this is acceptable for sheds. If you find ducking a problem, design a higher door opening. Standard door height, and that required by building codes for houses, is 6 feet, 8 inches.

If you choose a 6-foot, 8-inch door, size the header proportionate to the door width. If the door is 3x6 feet, 8 inches, the header should be made of two 2x4s, with their 4-inch sides nailed flush to increase the door's load-bearing capacity. On the other hand, if you are using two 3-

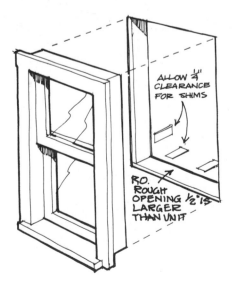

Figure 2.13—Double-hung window

foot-wide doors with no middle support, the 6-foot clear span requires a header made from two 2x8s nailed together. In either case, each end of the header must rest on a jack post, which in turn is nailed to a common stud. If you do decide to use the standard 6-foot, 8-inch door, the height of the shed walls will be at least 7 feet plus the floor thickness, or 7 feet 8 inches.

All that said, if you want the shed proportions wider than taller, your structure will be a minimum of 8 feet wide. To achieve the 3 to 4 ratio of width to length, your structure will have to be 10½ feet long.

Shed doors traditionally swing out, whereas residential doors generally swing in. The advantage to a door that swings out is that when the cold wind blows against it, it presses the door against the frame, thus minimizing air leaks.

Windows

Most sheds suffer from lack of interior light; in fact, the cheap metal sheds come with no windows at all. Looking for things in the dark can be frustrating. Homemade windows offer unlimited possibilities— everything from shutters (see page 65) to more elaborate handmade casements (see page 137) and typical shed windows (see page 128).

Factory-made double-hung windows can be purchased from your lumber-supply store and inserted into the rough window openings. Windows come in many styles—awning, casement and bays—but the most typical is the double-hung window (see Figure 2.13). These are always installed from the outside and nailed to the shed window framing. They come complete with casings, sills and hardware; however, they are expensive, and delivery can sometimes take weeks.

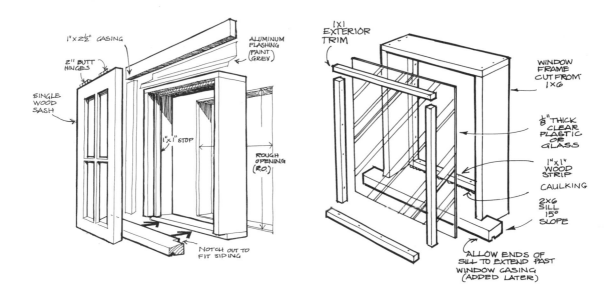

Figure 2.14—Hinged window and frame *Figure 2.14A—Fixed window*

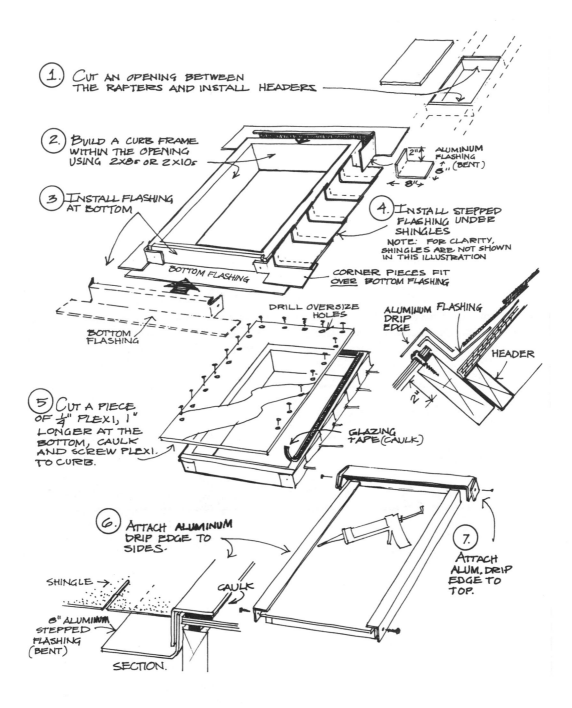

1. CUT AN OPENING BETWEEN THE RAFTERS AND INSTALL HEADERS

2. BUILD A CURB FRAME WITHIN THE OPENING USING 2X8s OR 2X10s

3. INSTALL FLASHING AT BOTTOM

BOTTOM FLASHING

BOTTOM FLASHING

2"
ALUMINUM FLASHING
6" (BENT)
8"

4. INSTALL STEPPED FLASHING UNDER SHINGLES
NOTE: FOR CLARITY, SHINGLES ARE NOT SHOWN IN THIS ILLUSTRATION

CORNER PIECES FIT OVER BOTTOM FLASHING

DRILL OVERSIZE HOLES

ALUMINUM FLASHING DRIP EDGE

HEADER

2"

5. CUT A PIECE OF ¼" PLEXI, 1" LONGER AT THE BOTTOM, CAULK AND SCREW PLEXI. TO CURB.

GLAZING TAPE (CAULK)

6. ATTACH ALUMINUM DRIP EDGE TO SIDES.

7. ATTACH ALUM. DRIP EDGE TO TOP.

SHINGLE

CAULK

8" ALUMINUM STEPPED FLASHING (BENT)

SECTION.

Figure 2.15—Skylight construction

Salvaged windows (See Figure 2.14) are an inexpensive alternative to factory-made windows and can often be found at your local dump free for the taking. Make sure you find them before you start building so that you know how big to make the rough openings. You can make these windows open by attaching hinges at the top.

Fixed windows (ones that cannot be opened) are another solution, and they are by far the easiest to make (see Figure 2.14A). Build a window frame out of 1 x 6 lumber and a 2 x 6 sloped sill. Attach a 1x1 stop around the inside of the frame, and set a piece of ⅛-inch clear plastic or glass against the stop in a bed of silicone caulking. Add four more pieces of 1 x 1 trim to the exterior side, and you are done.

For a description of a tilt-in window, see pages 128-129.

Skylights

Some shed builders object to giving up valuable wall space for windows, yet agree on the importance of shedding a little light on the interior. Skylights are a good solution. They allow in 30 percent more light than windows and offer a little warmth as well.

A factory-made skylight costs more than $100, and you still have to pay for installation or install it yourself. Here's a build-your-own skylight than can be built in less than one day by following the steps in Figure 2.15.

Standing inside the shed, use a framing square to locate and mark the four corners of your skylight; it must be located between two rafters. Hammer four long nails through the roof just inside the rafters where the corners will be. Outside, locate the nail points on the roof. Mark the perimeter of the skylight by snapping a chalk line from nail to nail. Remove the nails. From above, with the line as your guide, cut the hole with a circular saw or an electric jigsaw. Next, reinforce the top and bottom of the hole by nailing two headers between the rafters. Build a "curb" frame of 2x8s so it fits tightly against the headers and the rafters and protrudes about 2 inches above the roof. Caulk around the curb where it meets the roof.

Protect the skylight from leaks by installing 8-inch-wide aluminum flashing on all four sides. Cut several 10-inch pieces. Begin with the bottom of the skylight and work to the top. Bend each piece as shown, laying one side against the curb and the other side against the roof and under the adjacent shingle. Overlap the flashing, and staple each piece to the roof, placing the staple at the top edge, so that the overlapping piece of flashing covers the staple. Cover the top edge of the skylight with one piece of flashing, cut and bent as shown, making sure the top edge of the flashing fits well under the top row of shingles.

Cut a piece of ¼-inch Plexiglas 1 inch longer than the length of the curb, and drill ¼-inch holes 4 inches apart along the two side and top edges (not along the bottom edge). Lay a strip of glazing tape around the top edge of the curb, and lay the Plexiglas over it, so 1 inch extra overlaps the bottom. Using rubber washers and #8, 1-inch round-head screws, attach the Plexiglas to the curb. Do not tighten the screws too much or they will split the plastic. The oversize pilot holes that you drilled will allow for the expansion and contraction of the Plexiglas during temperature changes.

Finish the skylight by installing brown, aluminum drip edge along the sides and top to improve the appearance and protect the screw holes. Lay a generous bead of caulk before attaching the drip edge. Use only four screws, drilled through the side corners, to hold the drip edge in place. Notice that the top piece of drip edge goes on last.

Cutting Rafters

There are several ways to frame a shed roof. One is to build roof trusses on the ground and lift them into place (see Basic 8 x 10 Shed, pages 56-58). A more common method is to cut separate rafters and nail them to a ridgepole. Here are the basics:

On opposite ends of the shed, temporarily nail vertical 2 x 4 poles to the top and bottom plates. To ensure that the ¾-inch-thick ridgepole will be in the center of the shed, offset the poles by ⅜ inch.

Temporarily nail a 1 x 6 or 1 x 8 horizontal ridgepole to the 2 x 4 poles at the desired roof height. Stand back, check the height and angle. Adjust the height and slope by raising or lowering the ridgepole until it looks just right.

Using only two nails, tack a board in place so that the lower end barely covers the top 1½-inch plate and overlaps the ridgepole at the top. Inside the shed, mark where the top plate touches the lower end of the rafter, and mark where the ridgepole touches the rafter at the top (see Figure 2.16).

Remove the board and cut out the bird's-mouth notch (see Basic 8 x 10 Shed, Figure 3.14) and the angle at the top. Test its fit. Use this board as a pattern to trace the cuts onto all of the other rafters. Do not cut the bottom (tail) ends yet; wait until all the rafters are in place. Then mark them by snapping a chalk line across all of them and cut them all off at once. This insures that the fascia board will be perfectly straight.

Mark the height of the ridgepole on the temporary 2 x 4s and reposition it to extend beyond the gable for the overhang. Starting ¾ inch in from the outside edge, place a mark every 24 inches on center along both top plates and the ridgepole, then nail the rafters at the marks.

The plans in this book have a roof slope symbol: a triangle and two numbers. The horizontal line at the bottom of the triangle refers to the run and is always expressed in 12 inches. The vertical line of the triangle refers to the rise, which varies with the slope. To determine the roof height from the top of the top plate to the top of the ridgepole, divide the run by 12 and multiply by the rise. For example, if the slope is ⁹⁄₁₂ and the run (half the width of the shed) is 48 inches, divide 12 into 48 to get

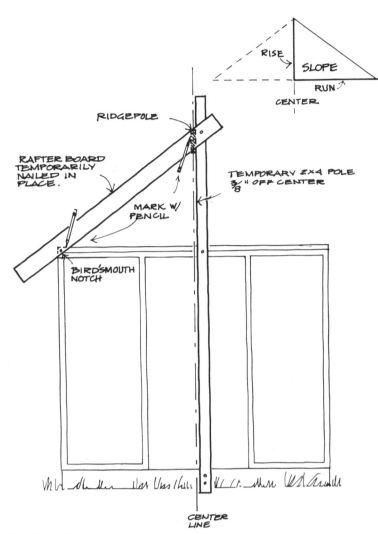

RISE

SLOPE

RUN

CENTER

RIDGEPOLE

RAFTER BOARD
TEMPORARILY
NAILED IN
PLACE.

MARK W/
PENCIL

TEMPORARY 2×4 POLE
3/8" OFF CENTER

BIRD'SMOUTH
NOTCH

CENTER
LINE

Figure 2.16—Cutting rafters

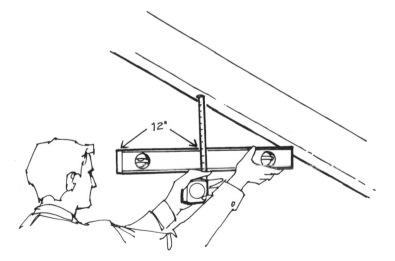

12"

Figure 2.17—Roof slope ratio

4, multiply 4 times the rise (which is 9) to get 36 inches.

To match a shed roof to a nearby building, take a level marked 12 inches from one end, place that end against the interior slope of the roof, and while holding it level, place a tape measure on the 12-inch mark. Extend the tape measure vertically until it reaches the roof and read the measurement from the roof to the level. This gives you the ratio of the slope (see Figure 2.17).

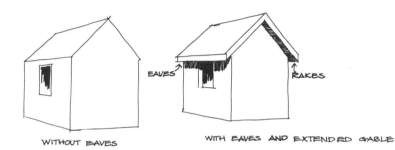

Figure 2.18—Eaves

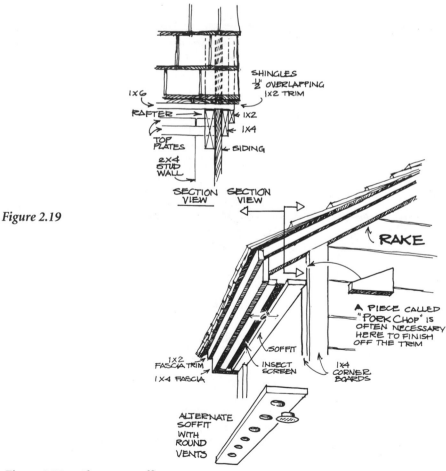

Figure 2.19

Figure 2.20—Alternate soffit

Eaves, Soffits and Rakes

Constructing the eaves, soffits and rakes may well be the most difficult task, but these often-overlooked architectural details make a shed look professionally crafted.

Eaves, the portion of the roof that hangs over the exterior walls, protect windows and walls from rain. Eaves complement the design and give the shed a more generous, substantial look (see Figure 2.18).

Soffits are the areas underneath the eaves, between the back of the fascia and the exterior wall. Soffits are important for ventilation and for preventing insects and squirrels from gaining access. Soffits can be designed in different ways (see Figures 2.19, 2.20).

Rakes are the gable-end version of eaves. A shed without rakes will save some time and material; however, in most cases, the roof appearance is much nicer if the rake overhang matches the eaves (see Figure 2.22). To accommodate rakes, you must extend the ridgepole and 2 x 4 look-out rafters to create a surface on which to nail the rake fascia. Lookout rafters are 2 x 4s notched into the end rafter and nailed into the next inside rafter, protruding out of the wall to meet the rake fascia (see

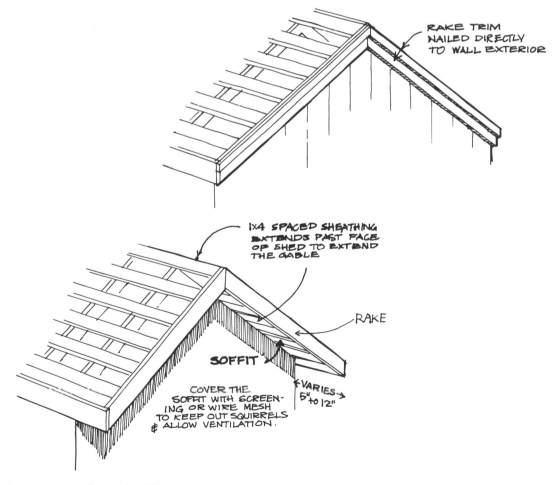

Figure 2.22—Rakes and soffits

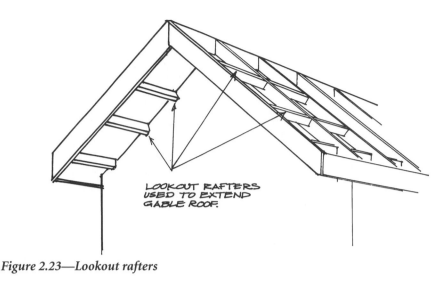

Figure 2.23—Lookout rafters

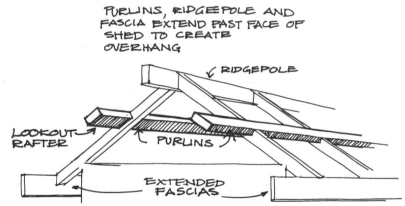

Figure 2.24—Alternate method of extending the gable

Figure 2.23). Make sure that the roof sheathing spans at least two rafters from the edge of the roof, so the edge will be well supported.

You can avoid framing-in a lookout rafter, if you are shingling your roof with wood shingles and are using spaced sheathing 1x4s for nailers. Simply order longer nailers and nail the rake fascia to the ends.

If you are using plywood as a base and want the rakes to overhang, another method is to run purlins across the width of the shed. This requires cutting notches in the rafters and installing a ridgepole (see Figure 2.24).

Slope and Types of Roofing

Slope is the slant or pitch of a roof as expressed in inches of rise to 12 inches of horizontal run. Most roofs are sloped in order to shed rain and snow. Obviously, the steeper the slope, the faster the runoff. Nearly flat roofs may develop areas in which the water rests, eventually causing a leak.

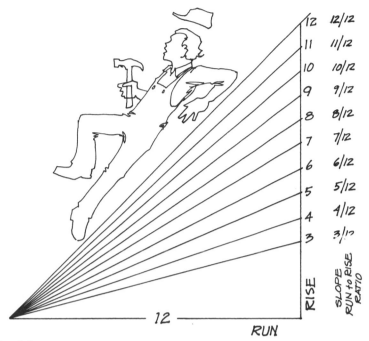

Figure 2.25—Roof slope

The angle of a double-sloped gable roof is determined by establishing a balance between the steepness necessary to shed rain, the economy of material, the amount of usable interior space and the difficulty of construction and repair. Another consideration is the slope of your house roof or other nearby building. If your shed is going to match the general style of the house, you would do well to use the house's roof slope for the shed as well, so that the roof lines complement each other.

Steeper roofs require longer rafters—more roofing material. Steeper roofs allow more usable space in the upper interior but are more difficult to repair. On the drawing board, a 30-degree or $7/12$ slope roof looks easy to walk on—when you are up there, it feels as though you are about to slide off it any moment. All things considered, the determining factor is usually aesthetics and most people prefer a slope of $7/12$ to $9/12$ slope. (see Figure 2.25)

A single-slope roof is a different matter. A shallow incline doesn't look out of place; in fact, a $3/12$ or $4/12$ slope might be perfect. Note that a $3/12$ slope will rule out the use of wood or asphalt shingles and will require rolled roofing.

Roofing choices are determined by aesthetics, location, climate and cost. Roofing materials vary from shingles, shakes and rolled roofing, to thatch and sod (see Figure 2.26). Cedar shingles generally look better than their asphalt counterparts, but they are more expensive and time-consuming to install. The most common length for cedar shingles is 18 inches, while hand-split shakes are generally 24 inches. Shakes vary in thickness and give a more rustic appearance to the roof. In either case, a slope of 4-inch/12-inch rise is necessary for proper runoff of rainwater.

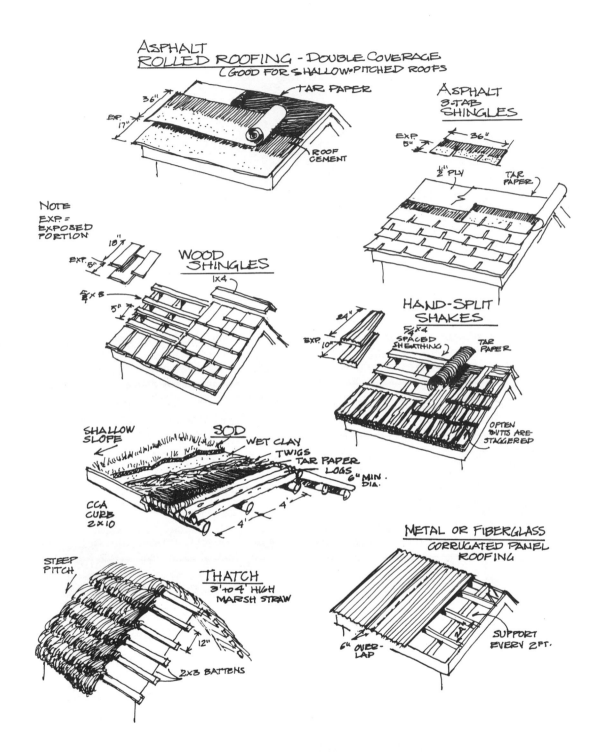

ASPHALT
ROLLED ROOFING - DOUBLE COVERAGE
(GOOD FOR SHALLOW-PITCHED ROOFS

TAR PAPER

36"

EXP.
17"

ROOF
CEMENT

ASPHALT
3-TAB
SHINGLES

EXP
5"   36"

½" PLY

TAR
PAPER

NOTE
EXP =
EXPOSED
PORTION

18"

EXT. 5"

5/8 X 8

WOOD
SHINGLES
1x4

5"

HAND-SPLIT
SHAKES

24"

EXP 10"

5/4 X 4
SPACED
SHEATHING

TAR
PAPER

OFTEN
BUTTS ARE
STAGGERED

SHALLOW
SLOPE

SOD

WET CLAY
TWIGS
TAR PAPER
LOGS

6" MIN.
DIA.

CCA
CURB
2x10

4'

4'

METAL OR FIBERGLASS
CORRUGATED PANEL
ROOFING

STEEP
PITCH

THATCH
3' to 4' HIGH
MARSH STRAW

12"

2x3 BATTENS

6" OVER-
LAP

SUPPORT
EVERY 2 FT.

Figure 2.26—Types of roofing

Eighteen-inch shingles require an exposed portion of 5½ inches, whereas 24-inch hand-split shakes should have 10 inches exposed to the weather (see Figure 2.27).

Shingling is a simple, effective system to cover the gaps between the shingles with the next course of shingles. The first course is doubled—one layer on top of another—and the second course is laid so that no joints line up with the preceding joints. In conventional house construction, saturated felt (tar paper) is used between the courses of hand-split shakes, however, in sheds this is unnecessary. The best base for wood shingles and shakes is 1x4 spruce sheathing. Space the boards 5½ inches on center for shingles and 10 inches on center for hand-split shakes or directly under the point where the shingle will be nailed. When nailing the 1x4 spaced sheathing onto the rafters, use a spacer made from scrap wood (see Figure 2.28).

Roofing shingles are figured by the "square," which is 10x10 feet or 100 square feet, and are sold by the bundle. It takes approximately four to five bundles of cedar shingles to cover a 10x10 square and six to eight bundles of hand-split shakes to cover a square. Both shingles and shakes should overlap the eave by 1¼ inch and the sides by ½ inch. Make sure that you nail on the fascia and the gable rakes before you start shingling. The gable rake trim is nailed directly to the ends of the 1 x 4 spaced sheathing. To insure that they line up correctly, snap a chalk line down the edges of the 1x4s and trim if necessary.

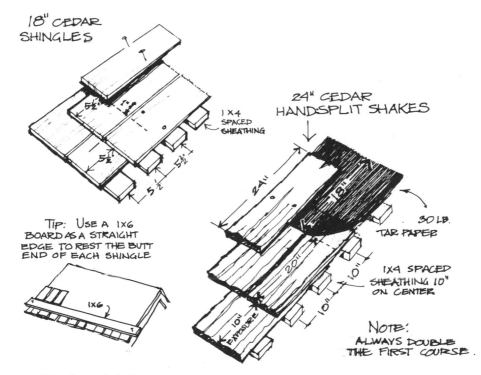

Figure 2.27—Shingles and shakes

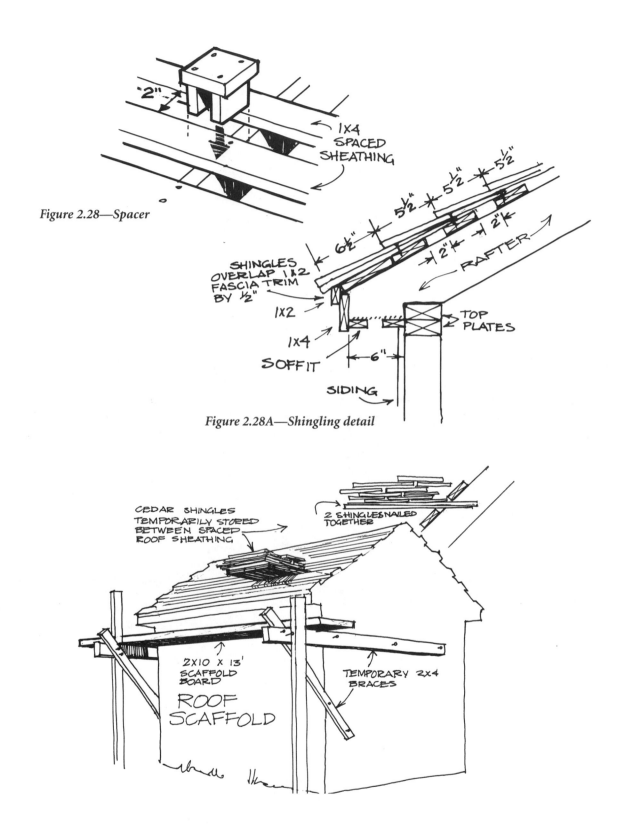

Figure 2.28—Spacer

"2"

← 1X4
SPACED
SHEATHING

5½" 5½" 5½"

6½" 2" 2" 2"

RAFTER

SHINGLES
OVERLAP 1x2
FASCIA TRIM
BY ½"

1x2

1x4

SOFFIT

6"

TOP
PLATES

SIDING

Figure 2.28A—Shingling detail

CEDAR SHINGLES
TEMPORARILY STORED
BETWEEN SPACED
ROOF SHEATHING

2 SHINGLES NAILED
TOGETHER

2X10 X 13'
SCAFFOLD
BOARD

ROOF
SCAFFOLD

TEMPORARY 2x4
BRACES

Figure 2.29—Holding rack for shingles

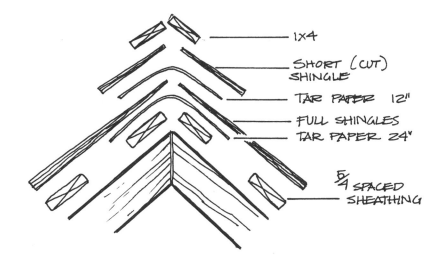

Figure 2.30—Ridge detail

Labels on figure:
1x4
SHORT (CUT) SHINGLE
TAR PAPER 12"
FULL SHINGLES
TAR PAPER 24"
5/4 SPACED SHEATHING

If you're considering plywood instead of spaced sheathing, realize that only spaced sheathing will allow ventilation for the shingles. Besides, the 1x4 boards are easier to handle and take almost the same amount of time to nail. And spaced sheathing creates a natural holding rack for the shingles when you work on the roof (see Figure 2.29).

The ridge is generally the most difficult part of a wood shingling job. It requires ripping and cutting shingles to the same width, using a table saw, and weaving them across the roof top. To make this easier, simply run the shingles up to the ridge, and lightly tack a heavy piece of 24-inch-wide tar paper that is folded in half, so that 12 inches hangs down on each side of the roof. Nail the next course of shingles over this and cut them off at the top, being careful not to cut through the tar paper. Tack on another 12-inch-piece of tar paper, folded to 6 inches on each side, and nail on the final course of shingles, using finishing nails (see Figure 2.30). Cut the shingles so that they protrude about ⅜ inch above the last course. When you shingle the other side, precut the last two rows so they butt up nicely under the shingles on the first side. If you don't like the rough edge this gives the roof, cap the ridge with two pieces of 1x4 nailed together.

For details on asphalt roofing, see the Basic 8x10 Shed, pages 63-64.

Cupolas

While small, decorative (nonfunctioning) cupolas can be ordered through most lumberyards for about $300 or more, the original intention of the cupola was to bring air, and sometimes light, into barns to prevent spontaneous combustion of the hay. Barn builders took great pride in creating their own designs, which explains why few cupolas are identical. You might want to add a cupola, and perhaps the traditional weather vane to your shed, just to improve the looks. A light shining

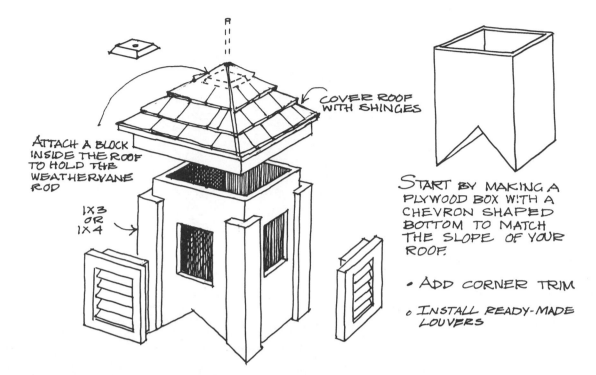

COVER ROOF WITH SHINGES

ATTACH A BLOCK INSIDE THE ROOF TO HOLD THE WEATHERVANE ROD

1×3 OR 1×4

START BY MAKING A PLYWOOD BOX WITH A CHEVRON SHAPED BOTTOM TO MATCH THE SLOPE OF YOUR ROOF.

• ADD CORNER TRIM

○ INSTALL READY-MADE LOUVERS

Figure 2.31—To make your own cupola

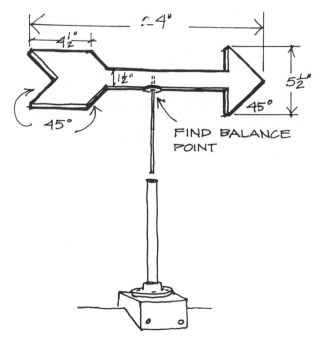

24"

4½"

1½"

5½"

45°

45°

FIND BALANCE POINT

Figure 2.32—Weather vane

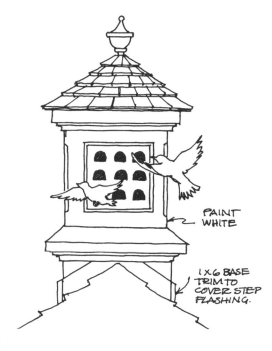

PAINT WHITE

1 X 6 BASE TRIM TO COVER STEP FLASHING.

Figure 2.33—Dovecote

through the louvers at night gives a nice effect. To make your own cupola, see Figure 2.31. The cupola width should be about one-eighth the length of the roof. If you install a copper cupola or weather vane, make sure it is grounded by connecting it to a copper wire that is buried several feet in the ground to protect the shed from lightning.

You can make your own weather vane out of ¾-inch-thick lumber (see Figure 2.32). Find the balance point and drill a ⅜-inch hole a few inches deep. Drill another hole on the top of the cupola and insert a ½-inch plastic pipe in it. Fit the top end of the rod loosely into the hole, enabling it to turn with the wind. Attach a block inside the roof to hold the weather vane rod.

Another type of cupola is the dovecote, popular in Europe during the fifteenth to seventeenth centuries when squabs were considered a delicacy by the feudal lords and helped sustain them during the winters when game was scarce. If you like the look of the dovecote, but don't relish the idea of pigeons roosting in your backyard, cover the holes with wire mesh (see Figure 2.33).

Insulation and Electricity

If you live in a cold climate and are planning to spend time in the shed in winter instead of just using it for storage, you may want to insulate and finish the inside and add electricity. However, these steps will add quite a bit more work to the construction job. There are several interior wall treatments to consider, including tongue-and-groove boards, sheetrock, plywood and wood paneling.

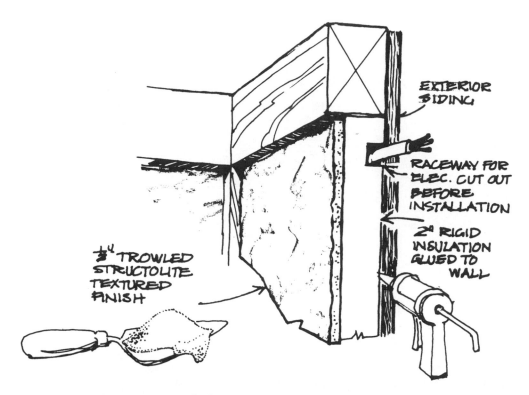

EXTERIOR SIDING

RACEWAY FOR ELEC. CUT OUT BEFORE INSTALLATION

2" RIGID INSULATION GLUED TO WALL

½" TROWLED STRUCTOLITE TEXTURED FINISH

Figure 2.34—Insulation

Fiberglass batts are the most common and inexpensive insulation option, if you are planning to finish the interior. They are certainly a wise option if you are insulating the floor.

An easier, more expensive solution is to cut, nail and glue panels of 2-inch rigid insulation to the interior wall and cover it with ½-inch trow-eled plaster-like stucco sold under the brand name "Structolite" (see Figure 2.34). Its pleasing appearance is also a fire retardant.

If your shed is framed in 2 x 4s, you will need to frame the inside corners to provide a nailing surface for the interior wall paneling. If you plan on heating the shed, insulate the ceiling and floor as well as the walls (see Figure 2.35).

To bring power and light to your additional abode, a 20-amp electrical circuit can be run underground 30 feet from your house by digging a 12-to-18-inch deep trench and burying a number 12 Romex housed in metal conduit. Most sheds will do with a single four-socket box, but if you are planning to operate many lights and tools, the shed should have its own panel box and circuit breakers sized according to the type of appliances or tools you plan to run. Experts recommend that you have a ground-fault circuit interrupter (GFCI) installed in the panel box. Check your local code for wiring requirements. Don't attempt any electrical work unless you are skilled in this area; do hire a professional if you are not.

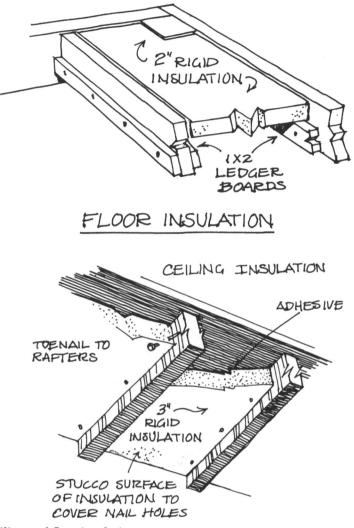

FLOOR INSULATION

CEILING INSULATION

Figure 2.35—Ceiling and floor insulation

Finishes

Finishes are necessary even to achieve the weathered look. All exposed wood will weather to a soft gray within a year—even sooner on the roof, since it is more exposed to the elements. For consistent color or a different color, stain or paint your shed. Exterior pine is best protected from mildew and rot with a coat of preservative.

Stain comes in solid, which hides most of the grain, and semi-transparent. Mix stains to create the desired shade. And you can accelerate the weathered look with bleaching oil followed by stain to preserve the appearance.

Paint is always an option. Any exterior paint is fine. Latex barn-red (or ranch-red) seems longest lasting.

Cedar roof shingles should receive a coat of sealer soon after installation. You can apply it easily with a garden sprayer.

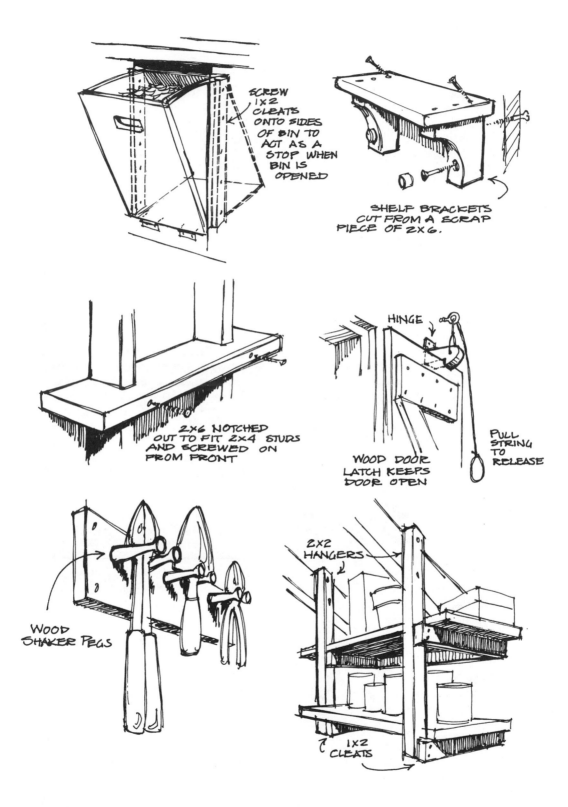

SCREW 1x2 CLEATS ONTO SIDES OF BIN TO ACT AS A STOP WHEN BIN IS OPENED

SHELF BRACKETS CUT FROM A SCRAP PIECE OF 2x6.

2x6 NOTCHED OUT TO FIT 2x4 STUDS AND SCREWED ON FROM FRONT

HINGE

WOOD DOOR LATCH KEEPS DOOR OPEN

PULL STRING TO RELEASE

WOOD SHAKER PEGS

2x2 HANGERS

1x2 CLEATS

Figure 2.36—Shelves and bins

Shelves, Bins, Hangers, Pegs, Etc.

Once the shed is built, you're ready for the interior features (see Figure 2.36). Refer back to your inventories and find or build a home for each item. For instance, you may want to build several shelves to store paint and household items. (To hang tools, you can buy all sorts of metal gadgets from your local hardware store, but the nicest ones are those that you make from wood so that they give a satisfying "clunk" sound rather than a "clang," when you hang up a tool.)

If it is a garden shed, build pullout bins for potting soil, fertilizer, mulch, lime and other garden supplies. Make a place for any poisonous chemicals out of the reach of children. Use the cross beams (collar ties) above to store items that are not regularly used, such as storm windows and lumber. One of the easiest things you can make to improve your shed is a door latch to keep the door from slamming closed in the wind.

Safety
Power Tools

- Always wear goggles or safety glasses when operating tools.
- Read all instructions carefully before using any power tools for the first time.
- Never operate a circular saw at a height over your head.
- When using a power saw, make sure the end of the piece of lumber that you're not using is *unsupported* and will fall away from the blade when cut through.

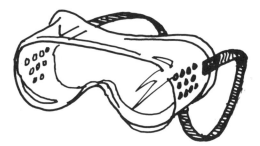

LADDERS

- Never put tools on top of a stepladder where you cannot see them from the ground.
- Never step on a ladder rung that is above the resting point of the ladder. This can put your weight on the other side of the fulcrum, making the ladder flip out from under you.
- Only use ladders on level ground. If the ground is sloped, dig holes for the uppermost legs.

Figure 2.37—Ladders

ROOFING

- Never underestimate the dangers inherent in working on a roof of any height. Make a scaffold by nailing metal roof brackets to the roof. Lay a scaffolding board (sold in lumberyards) over the braces and nail it temporarily in place (see Figure 2.38). Use a ladder to climb on the scaffolding. After removing brackets, fill nail holes with clear silicone.
- Always keep three body points touching the roof, i.e. foot, knee and hand. When you can no longer stand on the scaffolding and reach the area on which you are working, buy or rent brackets sold in the lumberyard made for this purpose (see Figure 2.38).
- Another type of scaffolding can be made by resting two sturdy 2 x 6s against the eave of the shed and attaching braces (see Figure 2.38).

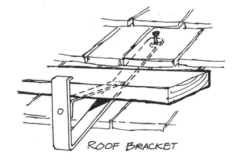

ROOF BRACKET

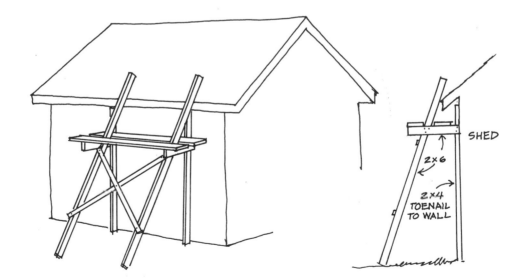

Figure 2.38—Scaffolding

Moving Sheds

Occasionally, you may need to build a shed in one spot and move it to another location, or you may simply need to move it to a new spot to make room for another building project. It is possible, with the help of a friend, to move a shed by hand, but it is much easier to use a vehicle, poles and a block and tackle to do the job. Be sure to empty your shed before moving it.

Buy three perfectly round poles, 10 feet long, from your lumberyard or farm-supply outlet. Jack up the shed and place two long boards under it to act as tracks, then slide two poles between the boards and the shed. Place two additional boards in front of and under the first two, and lay a third pole across them so that the shed will roll onto it. After tying a strong rope around the shed and attaching it to a vehicle with a trailer hitch, pull the shed slowly, removing the poles from the rear and placing them in front of the shed as it moves. If you don't have room to drive a truck to the new location, make a block-and-tackle rig as illustrated. Make sure that it is attached to a strong stump or tree (see Figure 2.39).

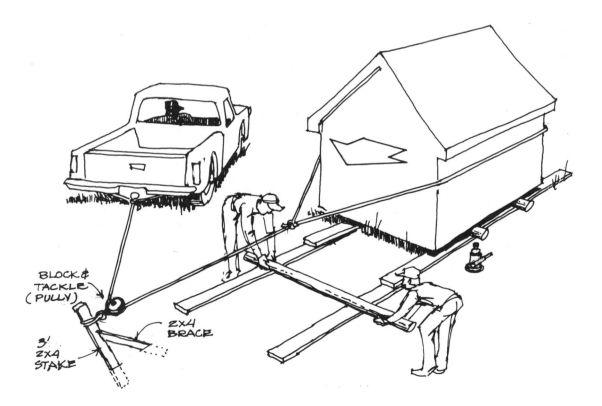

Figure 2.39—Moving a shed

Figure 3.1—Basic 8x10 Shed

CHAPTER 3

The Basic 8x10 Shed

A fter you've taken a careful look at your shed needs, your site and your budget, you may conclude that the classic 8x10-foot, versatile, multipurpose shed is perfect for you (see Figures 3.1–3.4). If you already own or can borrow the tools, you should be able to build this shed in about eight days.

This shed is big enough to store bikes, tools or garden equipment and will outlast any sheet metal shed you can buy. There are plenty of customized options to add later—shelving, bins or racks, whatever suits your tastes.

The shed is vertically sheathed in northern pine #2 construction grade, 1x10 shiplapped boards that cost about 62 cents a linear foot (1992 price). If northern pine is not available in your area, you may substitute 1x10 #2 shiplapped cedar, which, although more rot resistant, is more expensive (98 cents a linear foot in 1992). Other options are 1x8 tongue-and-groove cedar, texture #111 plywood or ½-inch CDX plywood, (the same material used to build most houses in the U.S.). Shingle the exterior walls later when you have more time.

The shed roof requires five bundles of asphalt shingles. If you prefer cedar shingles, expect to pay three times as much and allow more time to install them. Another option is to put on an asphalt shingle roof and cover it with a cedar shingle roof, which should last 15-30 years.

Materials Needed

Quantity	Description	Lengths	Location
Floor Framing			
4 minimum	solid concrete half-blocks	4x8x16 inches	corners
2	2x6 CCA	10 feet	joist frame
2	2x6 CCA	8 feet	joist frame
4	2x6	8 feet	joists
1	2x6 CCA	10 feet	center girder
3 sheets	¾-inch 4x8 CDX plywood		flooring
Wall Framing			
22	2x4 #2 constr. fir	6 feet	wall studs
2	2x4 " " "	10 feet	side-wall cats
2	2x10 " " "	10 feet	side-wall shelves
2	2x4 " " "	8 feet	end-wall cats
2	2x4 " " "	8 feet	end-wall shelves
6	2x4 " " "	8 feet	end plates
6	2x4 " " "	10 feet	side plates
3-4	2x4 " " "	10 feet	spare
Roof Framing			
6	2x4 #2 constr. fir	12 feet	roof rafters
6	2x4 " " "	6 feet	rafter collar ties
3	1x4 " " "	10 feet	temporary poles, trim
Sheathing and Siding			
4	½-inch CDX plywood	4x8	roof
26	1x10 shiplapped boards northern pine #2 construction grade	12 feet	walls & trim
Miscellaneous			
1	2x4 CCA	4 feet	door cap
2	1x4 northern pine #2	6 feet	window track
2	1x2 " " "	6 feet	window track
2	1x6 #2 pine or spruce	12 feet	fascia
4	1x6 " " " "	6 feet	gable fascia
4	1x2 " " " "	6 feet	gable fascia trim
3	⁵⁄₄ x 6-inch " " "	6 feet	door and shutter battens, Z-brace

Hardware

5 bundles asphalt shingles (charcoal) 3 tab
1 pair heavy-duty, 5-inch T hinges
1 door handle
3 lb. 10d common framing nails
1 lb. 8d common nails for flooring
3 lbs. 6d shake-ringed nails (for siding)
3 lbs. 1-inch, zinc-coated, ⅜-inch-head roofing nails
2 hooks & eyes (2-inch)

1 box 1½-inch deck screws
28 2½-inch deck screws
1 lb. 8d galvanized finishing nails
1 gal. solid gray stain (optional)
several pieces slate shims
22 feet 6x20-inch insect screen
1 tube premium caulking
1¼ x 2½-inch galvanized lag bolts and 2 washers

Tools Needed

16-oz. claw hammer	shovel
7½-inch portable electric saw with combo blade	16-lb. sledgehammer
24-inch crosscut hand saw	rake
¾-inch-wide measuring tape, 16 feet long	electric jigsaw or handsaw
	nail apron
framing square	8-foot ladder
utility knife	2 sawhorses
½-inch chisel	wrecking bar
chalk line & chalk	nail set
48- or 36-inch level	extension cord
carpenter's pencil	electric drill with Philips-head bit

Daily Schedule

DAY 1. PREPARATION

Order all the materials and have them delivered to your property in advance. Move the material to the actual building site. Gather all the tools that you will need and run an extension cord from the nearest outlet (making sure it is grounded). Decide exactly where you will put the four corner blocks and mark the spots.

DAY 2. GROUNDWORK AND FLOOR FRAMING

Prepare the site. Nail the floor frame together and attach the center girder. Cut and install joists. Cut and nail down ¾-inch plywood floor.

DAY 3. WALL FRAMING

Nail together the wall sections and erect them one at a time. Attach the top plate and "square up" the structure. Cut and nail cats between studs.

DAY 4. ROOF FRAMING AND SHEATHING

Build six trusses. Raise the two end trusses and attach the ridge support. Add the remaining four trusses. Cut and install plywood roof sheathing.

DAY 5. SIDING

Cut and nail siding to studs. Saw off protruding ends. Cut the door opening.

DAY 6. ROOFING, TRACK AND TRIM, FASCIA AND SHUTTERS

Build track and fascia. Install window shutters. Cut and fit fascia and trim. Cover roof with asphalt shingles.

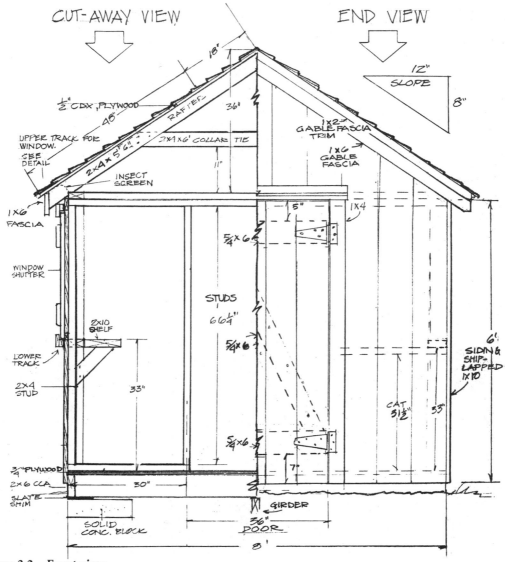

Figure 3.2—Front view

DAY 7. DOOR

Build and hang door. Install handle.

DAY 8. FINISH AND CLEANUP

Build shelf and ramp. Clean up. Admire work.

Step-By-Step Instructions

For starters, be organized in every way! For instance, decide where to keep your pencil and from then on, always return the pencil to the same pocket when you are finished using it. Do all your cutting in one place and throw your scraps in the same spot, so they don't get underfoot.

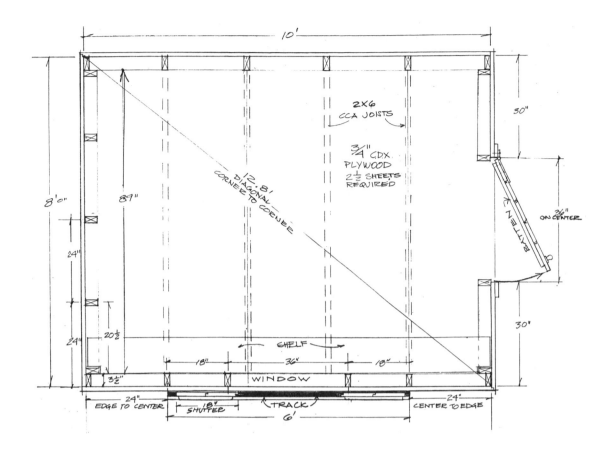

Figure 3.3—Floor plan

Begin by ordering all the material from your lumberyard (see Materials Needed), instructing the salesperson to write on the order exactly where you want the lumber unloaded. Mark off an area that is both convenient to your building site and accessible to the delivery truck (such as the end of your driveway). Do not expect the deliverer to hand-carry lumber to your building site—this is your job. Lifting and carrying a full sheet of plywood can be awkward and strenuous, so you may want to ask a friend to give you a hand. Arrange the lumber in a neat pile near your shed site, with the pieces you will use first on top. Keep the lumber off the ground by placing it on scrap pieces of 2x4s on edge or pallets. Lumber left on the bare ground will get dirty and could become infested with termites. It is not necessary to protect lumber from the rain. However, your tools should be stored in a safe, dry, easily accessible place.

Another important consideration is electric power. Although it is possible to make all the cuts using a hand saw, it is far easier to have electricity available at the site. This means bringing electricity out from the house by using a heavyweight extension cord that is grounded (three prongs) and has a multiple outlet.

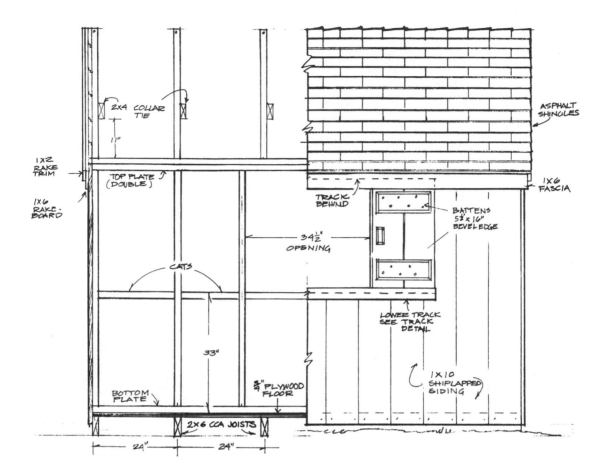

Figure 3.4—Side view

GROUNDWORK

For small sheds 8x10 feet or smaller, you do not need to stake out the corners to site the building. The nailed-together floor frame will mark the parameters. Begin by cutting 3 inches off the two 10-foot 2x6 rim joists to allow for the thickness of the other two boards. The finished frame should be exactly 8x10 feet (see Figure 3.5). Never trust the lumber you have bought to be *exactly* the length you ordered. Often lumber mills leave a little extra on the end for you to trim off.

Place one of the 4x8 sheets of plywood in the corner temporarily to determine the squareness of the frame, and tack the plywood to the frame to keep it square (see Figure 3.6). Then nail two temporary strips of wood diagonally across the frame to hold it square and remove the plywood. Finish nailing the four pieces together to form a frame for your floor joists. Temporarily lay the frame on the ground where you want the shed to be.

Starting with the highest point of ground, dig a trench about an inch deep around the frame for it to rest in. Since the lumber is pressure-treated, it will be all right to lay the frame directly on the ground. Next, dig a 3-inch-deep hole at the corner big enough to place a solid, concrete half-block underneath the corner of the frame, leaving about 3 inches of frame exposed. Set your level on the frame and adjust the height of the frame by propping it up with whatever is handy. Dig a shallow hole at the opposite corner from the first one and stack concrete blocks up until the frame is nearly level (see Figure 3.7). Use slate shims (which can be easily split) to bring the frame up to final level. Do the same for the other two corners, and you are ready for the floor joists (see Figure 3.8).

FLOOR FRAMING

Cut the four 2x6 pressure-treated CCA floor joists to fit inside the width of the frame, and nail them to the frame at 24-inch intervals, on center, flush with the top using 10d common nails.

For a *really* solid floor, place a 2x6 on edge lengthwise in the center of the floor frame. If necessary, trench out the earth underneath. Toenail the frame and joists to the girder (see Figure 3.9).

Lay two sheets of ¾-inch, 4x8 CDX plywood on top of the frame and nail them down using 8d (2½-inch) nails, nailing one about every 8 inches along each joist. Cut the third piece of ¾-inch plywood in half lengthwise, and nail one of the halves to the floor frame to complete the platform (see

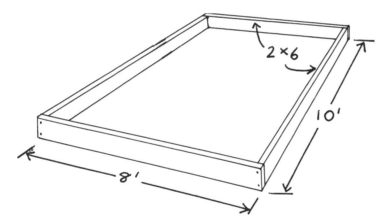

Figure 3.5—Floor frame

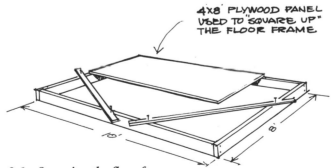

Figure 3.6—Squaring the floor frame

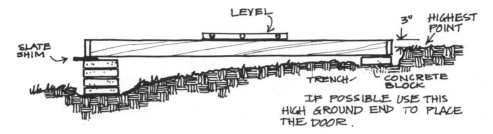

Figure 3.7—Leveling the frame

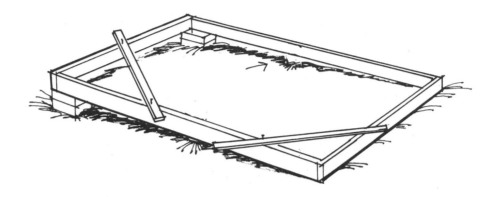

Figure 3.8—Bracing the frame

Figure 3.9—Floor joists

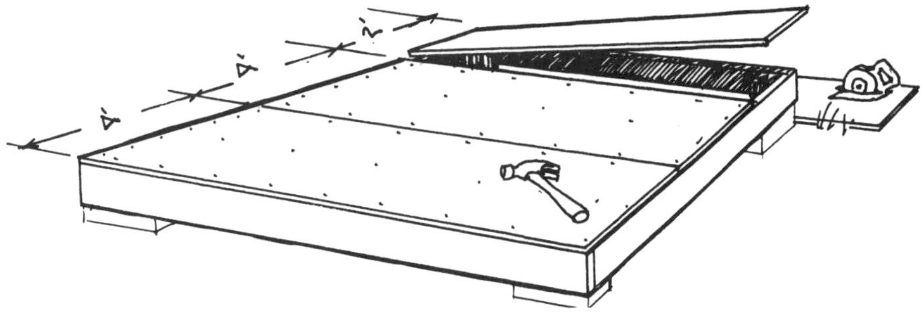

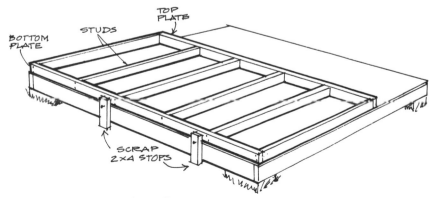

Figure 3.10—Floor

Figure 3.10). Save the remaining half sheet for the ramp. Test the floor for strength by jumping on it. If you don't feel a "buzz" in your feet, it is solid.

WALL FRAMING

This level platform on which to work will make it easier to frame the wall. Starting with the 10-foot wall, temporarily nail two scraps of 2x4 onto the outside edge of the platform frame to act as a brace. Lay a 10-foot 2x4 "on edge" on the platform against the brace. This will be the "sole" or bottom plate. Cut six 2x4 studs, 66¼ inches long, and position the interior studs at 24-inch centers. Lay a 10-foot 2x4 top plate along the top of the studs. Nail the top plate to the top of the studs and the bottom plate to the bottom of the studs. Prop the wall up, temporarily in place, and follow the same procedure for the remaining three walls (see Figures 3.11, 3.12).

By referring to the floor plan (see Figure 3.3) for dimensions, note that the wall with the door and the wall with the window have different positions for the studs. Don't worry that the door opening has a 2 x 4 plate along the bottom. Build it just like the other walls, with a continuous bottom plate, cutting the plate out with a handsaw later. Also, note that the two end walls are set in 3½ inches in order to allow for the thickness of the adjoining walls.

An easy way to make sure that the framing stays square is to temporarily nail panels of ½-inch plywood to the outside frame. Once the

Figure 3.11—Framing the wall

Figure 3.12—Raising the wall

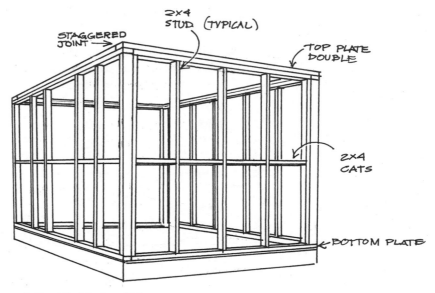

Figure 3.13—Finished wall frame

framing is square, nail the corners together and nail the bottom plate to the floor. Next, cut and nail the 2x4 cats (nailers) to fit between wall studs all around the perimeter to provide a nailing surface for the wall siding.

Finally, nail a top plate to the top of the structure, making sure to stagger the joints. This finishes the wall frame (See Figure 3.13).

ROOF FRAMING AND SHEATHING

Cut the six 12-foot 2 x 4s allocated for roof rafters into twelve 5½-foot lengths. Starting from the bottom, measure 6 inches and cut a bird's mouth notch 1 x 1½ inches. Then, measure 2⅜ inches from the top end, mark and cut off the end plumb (see Figure 3.14). Use this piece as a pattern to mark and cut 11 more rafters. Do not cut the bottom end of the rafter until they are all nailed in place. Then snap a chalk line 6 inches out from the face of the building along the top of the rafters and make a plumb cut straight down. This will allow the fascia to meet the ends of the rafters perfectly.

Place two rafters on the floor and place a spare 2x4, cut exactly 8 feet long, inside the bird's mouth of both rafters. This 8-foot 2x4 acts as a base to establish the width of the shed.

Place a 6-foot piece of 2x4 (collar tie) 11 inches above the base 2x4 and mark where it meets the rafters. Cut the ends off flush (see Figure 3.15). The collar tie must not extend past the rafters, or it will create a bump in the roof. Write the word "pattern" on these three pieces and use them as a template to mark the remaining trusses.

To build the trusses, screw the collar tie to the rafters, using 2½-inch deck screws and an electric screwdriver with a Phillips-head bit. Screw the peaks of the rafters together.

Raise the two end trusses by first nailing a temporary (1x4) pole 10 feet long, to the truss (see Figure 3.16). For a small shed like this one, one person can lift the truss into place. Nail the bottom half of the pole to the floor frame and top plates to help keep the truss plumb.

Once the two end trusses are in place, make a marking pole out of scrap lumber cut exactly 10 feet long. Mark, at 24-inch intervals, where

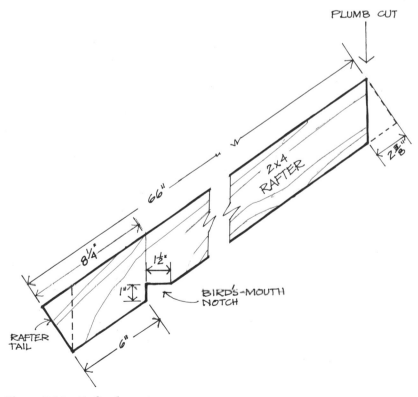

Figure 3.14—Rafter layout

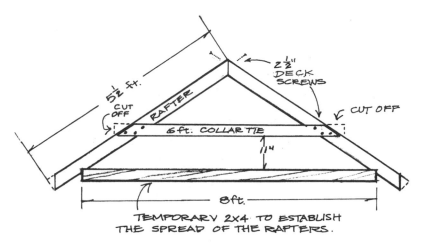

Figure 3.15—Adding the collar tie

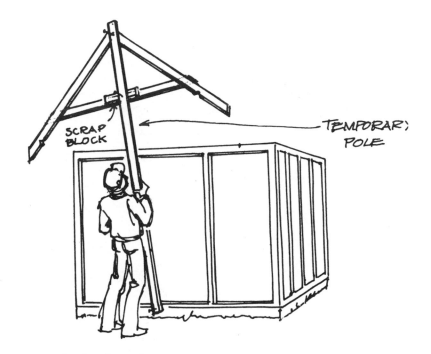

Figure 3.16—Setting the end truss

the peaks of the rafters will go. Temporarily nail the pole to the two end trusses. Lift the remaining trusses into position, and temporarily nail them to the marking pole (see figure 3.17).

To sheath the roof, starting at the peak, cut two 18x96-inch pieces from a full sheet of ½-inch CDX plywood. Nail these two pieces onto the top of the rafters, using 8d (2½-inch) common nails. Nail the first piece along the rooftop, remove the marking pole and nail the other piece along the top so the two edges meet. Nail the two full sheets of plywood directly below. The bottom edge will extend beyond the rafter ends by a

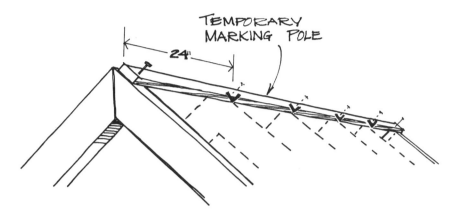

Figure 3.17—Roof framing

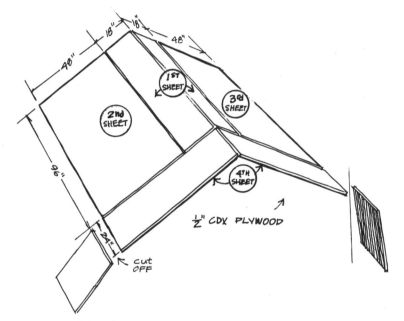

Figure 3.18—Roof sheathing

couple of inches. Cut the remaining piece of plywood in half lengthwise, and nail it to the roof. Cut off the overlap in line with the eave edge (see Figure 3.18).

SIDING

Before siding the shed, staple wire screen onto the top plate and under the rafters, to keep insects and squirrels out. Tack a 10-foot 2x4 to the base frame, its top edge level with the bottom edge of the plywood flooring. This acts as a straight edge on which the bottom of the siding can rest (see Figure 3.19).

Cut seven of the 12-foot 1x10 shiplapped boards into 6-foot lengths. Moving from right to left, nail these boards to one of the long sides of the shed—the one without the window. The tops should line up just

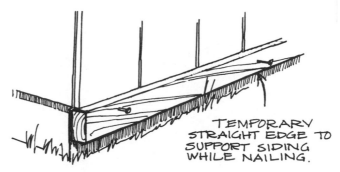

Figure 3.19—Siding support

under the rafters. Saw off any excess overlapping at the corner. Go back to the corner you started from and begin siding the adjacent gable end, working from left to right. Cut each board so that the end protrudes slightly above the edge of the gable. When that end of the shed is finished, snap a chalk line from the peak to the eaves and saw the protruding siding off (see Figure 3.21). Then move to the opposite corner from where you began and repeat the procedure for the other two walls (see Figure 3.20). Cut the siding to fit around the 34½-inch-wide window, but let it cover the door opening.

Consulting your plans, use a chalk line and straight edge to mark the location of the 36-inch-wide door. Make a line where the opening will be on center with 2x4 studs on each side. This allows the door frame to stop the door swing. The door height should be 71¼ inches; however, allow another 1½ inches at the top for the door cap. Mark this height. Set the electric saw blade depth to the thickness of the siding. Check the diagonals for squareness, then cut the door opening (see Figure 3.21).

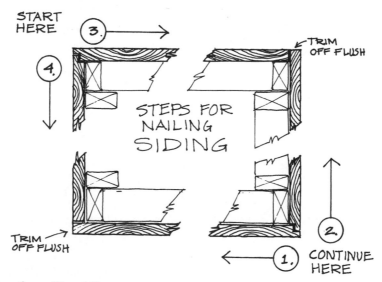

Figure 3.20—Steps for nailing siding

Figure 3.21—Door opening

Cut the beveled door cap from a piece of 2x4 CCA. With a block plane or a table saw, bevel the top to an 8-degree angle. (see Figure 3.22). Notch the ends to fit around the siding, then screw on the door cap from underneath. Caulk the top seam with premium adhesive caulking.

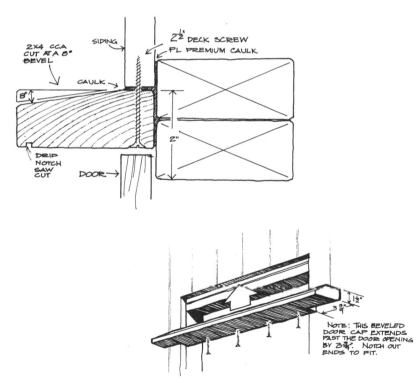

Figure 3.22—Beveled door cap

TRACK AND TRIM

The track that holds the shutters must be installed before the trim, since there will not be enough room to swing a hammer once the fascia is on. Cut and fit a piece of 1x4 (track support) into the top 34½ inches of the window opening and nail it to the top plate. Nail a 1x4 and a 1x2, each 6 feet long, together to form an L-shaped track for both the top and bottom. Using a strip of asphalt roofing shingle as a spacer, nail the tracks to the wall. The spacer allows the shutters to slide easily (see Figure 3.23) to reveal the open window (this is not a glass window).

To begin the gable trim, mark and cut four pieces of 6-foot 1x6s. Temporarily tack them to the gable edge so that they overlap at the top. Mark them and cut them off to match. Then cut the tail ends flush with the rafter ends. Next, temporarily nail up the two 1x6 12-foot side fascia boards. Mark where they extend past the gable fascias and cut off the ends. Nail on all the trim, using 2½-inch galvanized finishing nails. Mark, cut and fit the outside 1x2 gable trim so it overlaps the side fascia (see Figure 3.24). Finally, cut two pieces of 1x4 and nail them to the sides of the door opening.

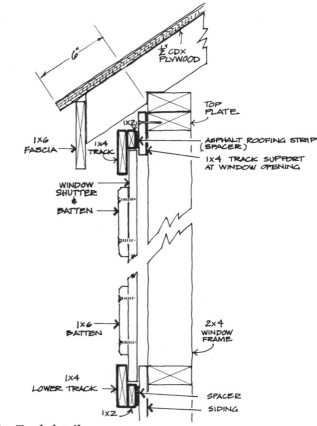

Figure 3.23—Track detail

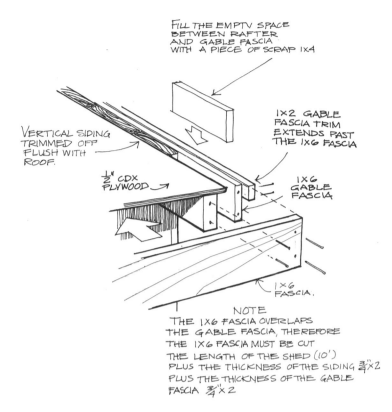

FILL THE EMPTY SPACE
BETWEEN RAFTER
AND GABLE FASCIA
WITH A PIECE OF SCRAP 1X4

1X2 GABLE
FASCIA TRIM
EXTENDS PAST
THE 1X6 FASCIA

VERTICAL SIDING
TRIMMED OFF
FLUSH WITH
ROOF.

1X6
GABLE
FASCIA

½" CDX
PLYWOOD

1X6
FASCIA.

NOTE
THE 1X6 FASCIA OVERLAPS
THE GABLE FASCIA, THEREFORE
THE 1X6 FASCIA MUST BE CUT
THE LENGTH OF THE SHED (10')
PLUS THE THICKNESS OF THE SIDING ¾"X2
PLUS THE THICKNESS OF THE GABLE
FASCIA ¾"X2

Figure 3.24—Fascia and rake

ROOFING

Today's house builders recommend installing an aluminum drip
edge along the gable side of the roof and an aluminum eave drip
edge along the eave side as precaution against water infiltration.
They also recommend covering the roof with 15-pound tar paper before
applying the shingles. Generally this is good advice; but since this is
a small shed and not a living space, these two steps can be eliminated.

Before setting foot on the first step of the ladder, it is a good time to
be reminded of the safety tips on pages 42-43.

To start the roof, create a base for the first row of shingles by nailing
on a starter course of shingles upside down with the tabs (slots) pointing
toward the peak. Nail the starter shingles to the front edge of the roof,
allowing a ⅜-inch overhang.

Next, cover the starter shingles with a row of shingles facing with
the tabs down. Since each three-tab shingle is 3 feet wide, it will take
four shingles to complete one row. Allow 1¾ inch to extend over the
gable edge. This will provide for the trim when it is installed later. Nail
four ⅜-inch-head galvanized roofing nails ⅝ inch above the slots of
each shingle. Before starting the next row, cut the first shingle in half
so that the cut-outs are staggered from row to row. Each row must be
offset by one-half a tab from the preceding row so that the slots do not
line up (see Figure 3.25). Each row of shingles should be 5 inches
above the preceding one. You can make this easier by snapping a chalk

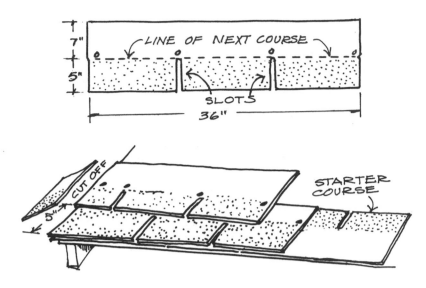

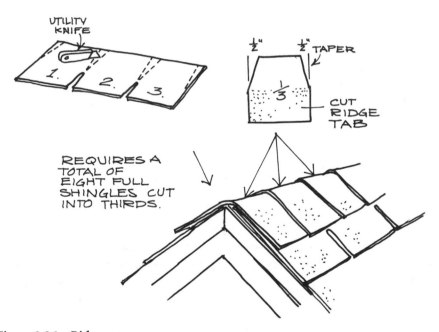

Figure 3.25—Shingling

Figure 3.26—Ridge cap

line 5 inches above the lower edge of the last row installed, then butting the edges of the next course along the chalk line. Once you have put on six or seven rows, measure from the ridge to see if the rows are even. If they are not even, adjust each remaining row slightly in order to finish evenly at the top.

Repeat for the other side of the roof.

The ridge will require eight shingles, each cut into three pieces. Taper the top portion of the shingle so the edges will be hidden (see Figure 3.26). Starting from one end, bend each tab over the ridge and secure with two nails each.

SHUTTERS

Cut four pieces of 1 x 10 30½ inches long and four pieces of 1 x 6 16 inches long for the battens. If you have access to a portable table saw (or hand plane), bevel the batten edges 45 degrees. Join the shutter pieces in pairs, and screw the battens to them with 1⅛-inch screws. Slide the shutter in from the side of the tracks. Attach two 2 x 4-inch handles by screwing them on from behind. Install two hooks and eyes on the inside so that the shutters can be opened only on the inside (see Figure 3.27).

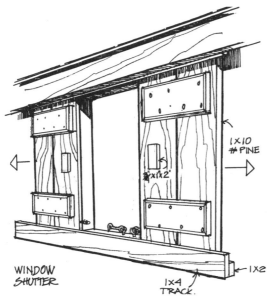

Figure 3.27—Shutters

DOOR

You can assemble the 36-inch-wide door from the pieces of siding you cut out to make the door opening. Fit the pieces squarely together and trim to a length of 6 feet. The ¾-inch exposed part of the door frame acts as a doorstop, so the door battens should be 34½ inches long, leaving a ¾-inch space on each side. Mark 5 inches down from the door top and attach a ⁵⁄₄ x 6-inch (square edge) batten, using 1½-inch screws. Measure 7 inches up from the bottom and attach the batten. Cut a ⁵⁄₄ x 6 to a 5-foot length. Position it diagonally across the battens to mark the angles. Make sure it runs from the outside bottom corner of the top batten to the bottom hinge to form a Z-brace. Cut and attach with screws.

Install the door flush with the exterior trim for an unobstructed swing outward so that when the wind blows, it will press inward against the stop. Using a foot prop, screw the 5-inch heavy-duty T-hinges to the battens and trim. Attach a handle and a door turn-latch (see Figure 3.28) 36 inches from the floor. Make the turn latch from a scrap of 1 x 2. Round the corners and drill a ¼-inch hole in the center. Install it using a ¼ x 2½-inch lag bolt and washers.

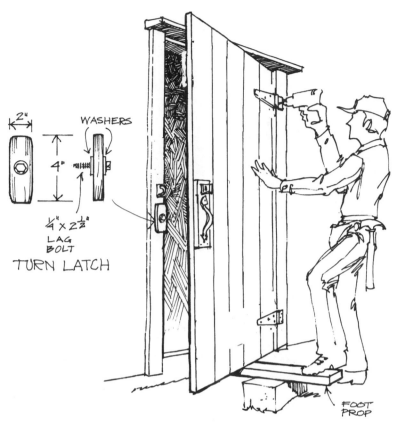

Figure 3.28—Door

SHELF

Cut a piece of 2x10 long enough to rest on the 2x4 cats on each end of the shed. Cut a 1½x3½-inch notch from each end of the shelf to allow for the framing. Cut two 15-inch-long 2x4s with a 45-degree angle at each end. Nail these braces to the studs and toenail them to the underside of the shelf (see Figure 3.29).

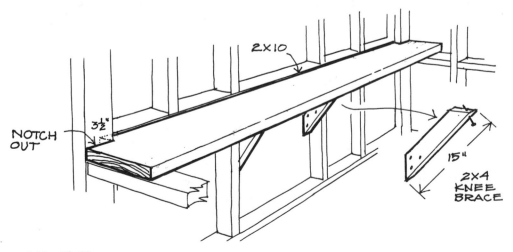

Figure 3.29—Shelf

RAMP

From one 48-inch-long 2x4, make a diagonal cut to form two wedge-shaped pieces for the footing of the ramp. Cut the remaining leftover piece of ¾-inch plywood flooring in half. Nail the two pieces of plywood to the wedge-shaped pieces. Slide the ramp into place so that the back is underneath the door and against the shed (see Figure 3.30).

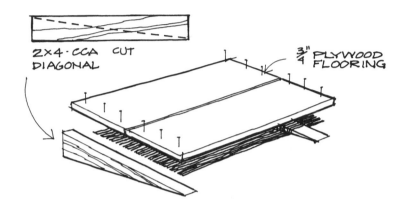

2X4·CCA CUT
DIAGONAL

¾" PLYWOOD
FLOORING

Figure 3.30—Ramp

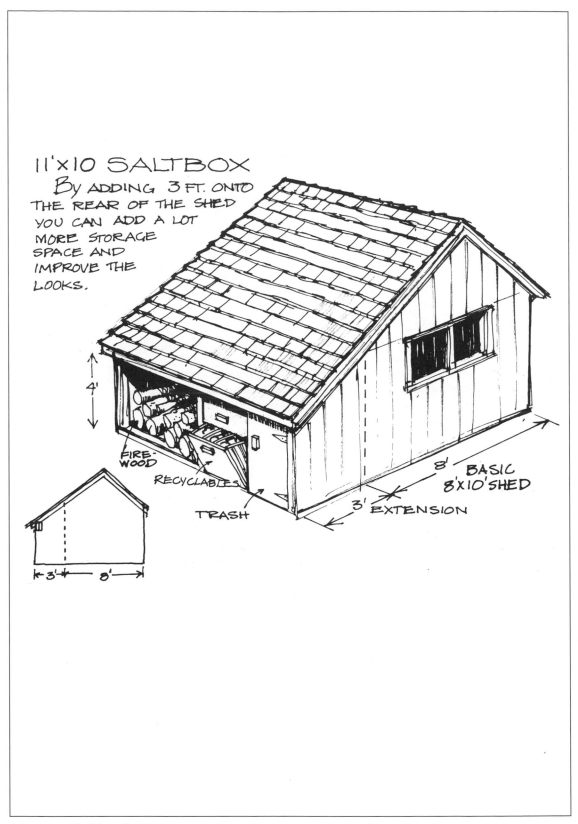

11'x10 SALTBOX

By adding 3 ft. onto the rear of the shed you can add a lot more storage space and improve the looks.

4'

FIRE-WOOD

RECYCLABLES

TRASH

8' BASIC 8'x10' SHED

3' EXTENSION

3'   8'

Figure 4.1—Saltbox Shed

CHAPTER 4

More Basic Sheds

&

11 x 10 Saltbox Shed

This saltbox variation (see Figure 4.1) adds a shed roof and a window to the original Basic 8x10 Shed design. Follow the steps of the Basic 8x10 Shed in Chapter 3 through the section on Roof Framing and Sheathing on pages 56-59. Before sheathing the roof, add the saltbox portion of the roof.

This roof is altered by adding 4 feet to one leg of each pair of rafters, forming a long overhang on one side of the shed. Bury two 4x4 CCA posts below the frost line at each corner, and join them to the shed with 2x4s toenailed to the top and bottom of each post. Install another 4 x 4 CCA post between the corner posts to support the rim joist, which is made from two pieces of 2x6 nailed together.

The end window is a shortened version of the wraparound window described on page 70.

Use this 3x10-foot extra space created in the saltbox shed to store any-thing—firewood, trash, recyclables, outdoor games, bicycles or lumber.

8 x 10 Shed With Wraparound Windows

This variation on the Basic 8 x 10 Shed features easily made fixed windows that wrap around three sides of the shed (see Figure 4.2).

Complete the Basic 8 x 10 Shed through the section on Floor Framing on pages 53-56. Instead of following the Wall Framing instructions in that chapter, frame the walls with 2 x 4 studs placed at 2-foot intervals on center. Install horizontal cats 4 feet from the floor.

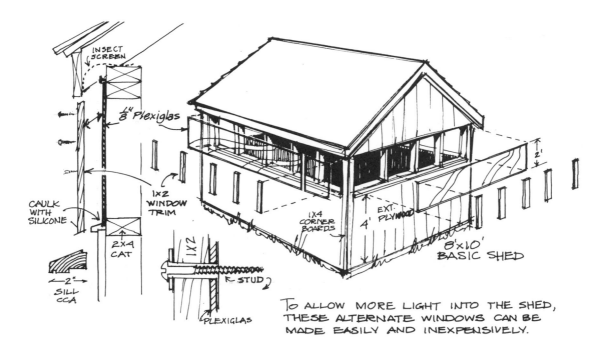

Figure 4.2—Wraparound windows

Cover the walls with 4 x 4-foot ⅝-inch exterior plywood texture #111.

With a table saw, cut the sill pieces from 2 x 4 CCA, and install them as shown in Figure 4.2.

Next, buy two 4 x 8-foot sheets of ⅛-inch-thick Plexiglas and ask that it be cut into 2-foot-wide strips. Have one of the strips cut into two 2-foot lengths (2 x 2 feet square), leaving you with a 2 x 4-foot scrap.

Install the Plexiglas by embedding the ridges in clear silicone. Hold it in place with pieces of 1 x 2 window trim. Since you can't screw through Plexiglas, first drill oversized holes (using a ¼-inch drill) through both the 1 x 2s and the Plexiglas as illustrated. Attach the 1 x 2s and the Plexiglas to the shed with a screw and washer (see Figure 4.2). Caulk wherever necessary. Build the rest of the shed following directions for the Basic 8 x 10 Shed. You will end up with a shed whose bright interior encourages you to work inside and enables you to find things easily.

Figure 4.2A—Garden-Tool Shed

Simple Garden-Tool Shed

This garden-tool shed is easy enough to construct in one day. It attaches to the house and provides a dry storage area where you can keep all your garden tools in one place. There is room for rakes, shovels, pots, fertilizer, gardening boots, a weed eater and even a small lawn mower. Because the shed rests against the wall of your house, it looks best if you build it out of materials that match or are at least compatible with your house. For simplicity, we have specified exterior-grade plywood; however, you could also use grooved-texture 111 fir plywood or cedar plywood. A 9-inch-deep shelf near the top of the shed can be used to store chemicals, as it is high enough to be out of reach for children. Pegs hold smaller garden tools such as trowels, shears and pruners.

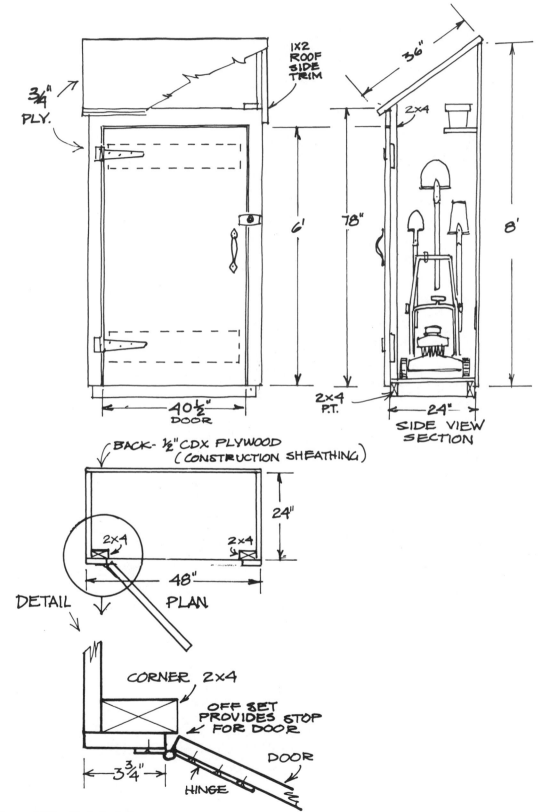

3/4" PLY.

1X2 ROOF SIDE TRIM

6'

40½" DOOR

78"

36"

2×4

8'

2×4 P.T.

24"

SIDE VIEW SECTION

BACK- ½" CDX PLYWOOD (CONSTRUCTION SHEATHING)

24"

2×4

2×4

48"

DETAIL

PLAN

CORNER 2×4

OFF SET PROVIDES STOP FOR DOOR

DOOR

3 3/4"

HINGE

Figure 4.2B—Tool shed plans

MATERIALS

1 4 x 8-foot sheet ¾-inch exterior plywood for front
1 4 x 8-foot sheet ½-inch CDX plywood for back
1 4 x 8-foot sheet ¾-inch exterior plywood for sides
1 12-foot 2x4 for base
1 4 x 8-foot sheet ¾-inch exterior plywood for floor and roof
1 6-foot 1x2 of #2 pine for roof trim
1 14-foot 2x4 of #2 pine for corners
1 6-foot 1x6 of #2 pine for door batten
1 5-inch door handle
1 pair 8-inch strap hinges for door
shingles to match house

STEP-BY-STEP INSTRUCTIONS

To make the shed floor, cut a piece of ¾-inch plywood to 24 x 46½ inches. Make a support frame for the floor by cutting two 21-inch pieces of 2x4 and two 46½-inch pieces of 2x4 and screwing them together. Nail the plywood over the support frame (see Figure 4.2C).

Cut two 24-inch-wide side panels out of ¾-inch plywood, 78 inches high at the front and 96 inches high at the back. Be sure to position the plywood so that the portion to be cut off is unsupported and will fall away from the outside edge of the blade. This is important because it helps prevent the saw from pinching and bucking back (see Figure 4.2D).

Nail the full sheet of ½-inch plywood to the back edge of the two sides, and nail the sides and back to the base (see Figure 4.2E).

Turn the assembly over. Cut a piece of ¾-inch plywood 77ž x 48 inches, and nail it to the front. Measure, mark, and cut out the door panel from the front piece of plywood, 3¾ inches from each side edge and 6 feet up from the bottom edge (see Figure 4.2F).

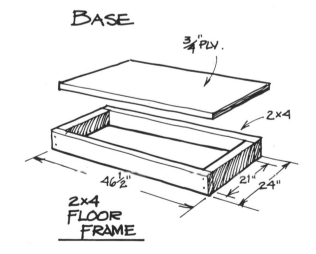

Figure 4.2C—Floor frame

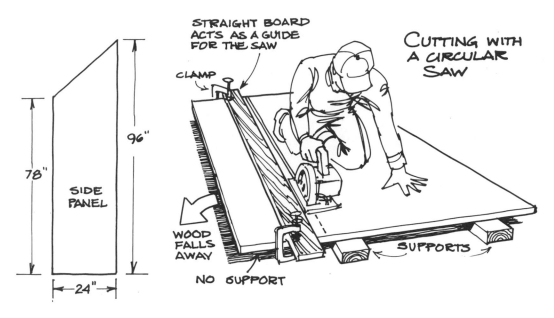

STRAIGHT BOARD
ACTS AS A GUIDE
FOR THE SAW

CUTTING WITH
A CIRCULAR
SAW

CLAMP

96"

78"

SIDE
PANEL

WOOD
FALLS
AWAY

NO SUPPORT

SUPPORTS

←—24"—→

Figure 4.2D—Cutting side panels

Turn the door panel over, and nail two 36-inch 1x6 battens 6 inches from the top and bottom edges of the door (see Figure 4.2G).

To reinforce the door frame, nail a 77-inch 2x4 into each inside front corner. Allow each 2x4 to protrude ½ inch into the door opening to act as a stop for the door when it swings in (see Figure 4.2H).

Lay the assembly on its back, and screw on the hinges, door handle and turn latch (see Figure 4.2I). To make the latch, cut a 3-inch piece of 1x2, and round off the corners with sandpaper. Drill a $^5/_{16}$-inch hole in the center, and screw a ¼ x 3-inch lag screw (and washer) through the

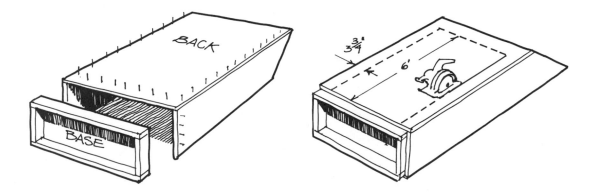

BACK

BASE

3/4"

6'

Figure 4.2E—Basic assembly

Figure 4.2F—Door panel

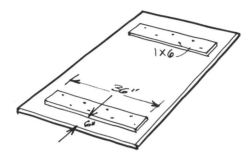

Figure 4.2G—Attaching hardware

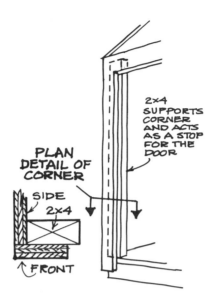

Figure 4.2H—Reinforcing door frame

hole and into the door frame. Adjust the tightness of the screw so that the latch stays in place when turned.

Cut and nail a piece of 36 x 48-inch ¾-inch plywood to the top of the shed, and nail a piece of 1x2 trim onto each side (see Figure 4.2J).

Use the leftover piece of plywood to make a 9-inch-deep shelf that you nail in place from the outside of the shed (see Figure 4.2J). Cover the roof with the same type of roof covering as your house (see pages 31-33 for types of roofing).

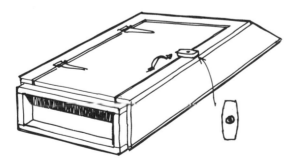

Figure 4.2I—Attaching hardware

Figure 4.2J—Attaching trim

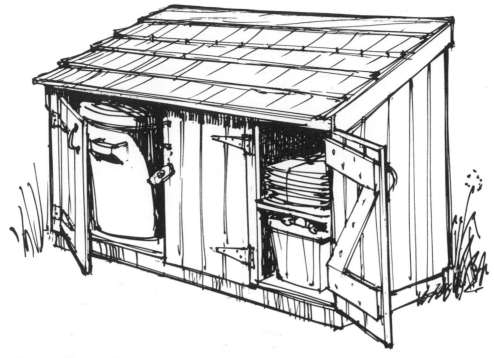

Figure 4.3—Recycling Shed

Recycling Shed

Here is a place for all the recyclables you have been trying to cram elsewhere (see Figures 4.3 and 4.4). This little shed will hold two 32-gallon trash cans, a plastic container for bottles and cans and a shelf for newspapers. The 6-foot-wide, 30-inch-deep and 4-foot-high shed is made of long-lasting cedar. The base is pressure-treated lumber. It can be built in one weekend and can be either freestanding or attached to an existing wall.

Since recycling requirements are ever-changing and vary in different parts of the country, I have designed a basic shed that can be altered. For instance, if you need to separate green from clear glass, simply add shelves to another one of the compartments, instead of filling it with a garbage bin. Attach plastic receptacles on the shelves as bins to store different colored glass bottles.

MATERIALS

½-inch exterior plywood
1x6 shiplapped cedar boards
2x4 CCA for base frame
2x4s for framing
1x4 CCA for flooring
¾-inch plywood for shelf
1x2s for stop and shelf supports
1x4 #2 pine for trim & door battens

18-inch cedar shingles
3 galvanized handles
3 pairs 5-inch hinges
5½ x 4-inch lag bolts
8d common nails
3-inch galvanized deck screws
1-inch deck screws
stain (optional)

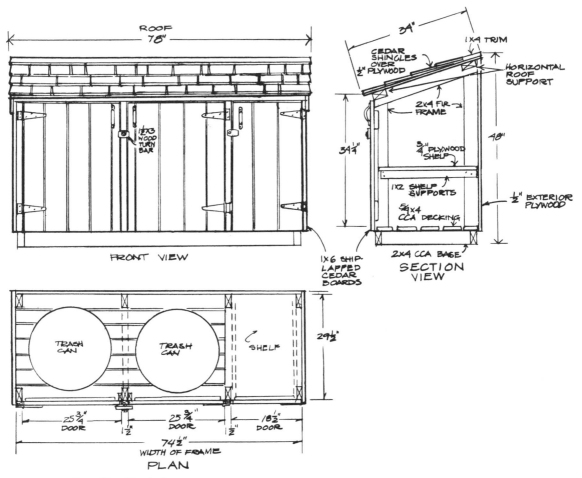

Figure 4.4—Recycling Shed plan

STEP-BY-STEP INSTRUCTIONS

Prepare a 6 x 3-foot area at the site by taking out any vegetation, stones, roots, etc. Level the ground by removing soil from the high spots and adding it to low areas and shimming low spots with stones or slate.

Build the floor frame out of two CCA 2x4s 71½ inches long for the front and back, two 29½-inch 2x4s for the sides and two 26½-inch 2x4s for the inside floor joists (see Figure 4.5). Install the 1x4 CCA spaced flooring flush with the outside edge of the base.

Lay two 4-foot pieces of 2x4 on the ground, 29½ inches apart. Temporarily lay a 36-inch piece of 2x4 on top of them at an angle that has one end flush with the 2x4 and the other 34¼ inches from the end. Mark the 2x4s (see Figure 4.6) where the top rafter overlaps the posts. Remove the rafter, and using a scrap of 2x4 as a template, mark where the horizontal roof support notches should go. Also, mark where the rafter will join the posts. Saw bird's-mouth notches to accept the horizontal roof supports and notch out the rafter so that it fits over the top of the rear post. Using these pieces as patterns, cut the three other rafters, and screw the frame to the floor.

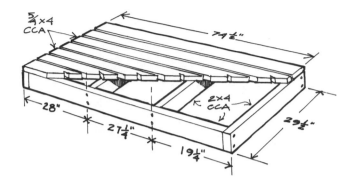

Figure 4.5—Recycling Shed base frame

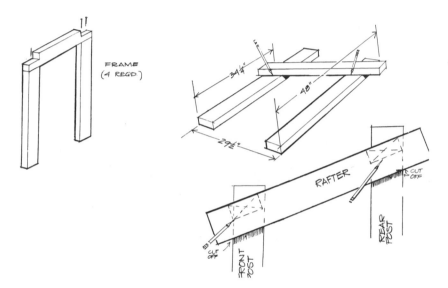

Figure 4.6—Recycling Shed wall frame

For horizontal roof supports, cut two 2x4s, 74½ inches long, and screw them into the notches you cut.

Cut and nail a ½-inch-thick sheet of exterior plywood to the back and top.

Panel the side walls and make doors of 25¾-inch, 1x6 shiplapped cedar. Cut and nail 1x2s to the front face of the 2x4 frames. Screw 1x4 battens to the back of the doors using 1-inch deck screws and attach them with 5-inch hinges.

Cut the shelf or shelves from ¾-inch plywood and install using 1x2s as shelf supports.

Install the handles, wood turn-bolt, and, if you wish, paint the shed with transparent stain.

Figure 4.7—Firewood Shed

Firewood Shed

This sturdy woodshed (Figure 4.7) should withstand the test of time. Constructed largely of rot-resistant CCA southern pine, the walls are made of boards spaced 1 inch apart, allowing air to circulate to the interior. A south-facing woodshed brings in maximum sunlight to season the firewood. The woodshed is 8x8 feet and will hold more than a cord of wood.

STEP-BY-STEP INSTRUCTIONS

Bury the ends of six CCA 4x4 8-foot posts 30 inches into the ground as shown on the plan (see Figure 4.8), with rear posts 8 feet apart and the two side posts 6 and 8 feet in front of the rear posts, respectively.

Nail diagonal 2x4 CCA braces to the front and rear posts as shown in

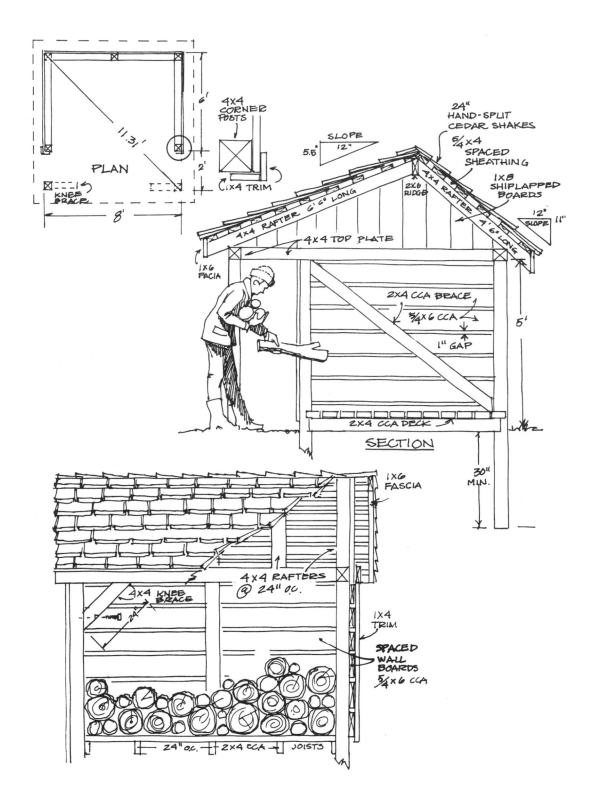

PLAN

6'

4X4
CORNER
POSTS

11.3'

2'

1X4 TRIM

KNEE
BRACE

8'

SLOPE
5.5" / 12"

24"
HAND-SPLIT
CEDAR SHAKES

5/4 X4
SPACED
SHEATHING

1X8
SHIPLAPPED
BOARDS

4X4 RAFTER 6'6" LONG

2X6
RIDGE

4X4 RAFTER 4'6" LONG

12"
SLOPE
11"

4X4 TOP PLATE

1X6
FACIA

2X4 CCA BRACE

5/4 X6 CCA

1" GAP

5'

2X4 CCA DECK

SECTION

30"
MIN.

1X6
FASCIA

4X4 KNEE
BRACE

24"

4X4 RAFTERS
@ 24" O.C.

1X4
TRIM

SPACED
WALL
BOARDS
5/4 X6 CCA

24" O.C.   2X4 CCA   JOISTS

Figure 4.8—Firewood Shed plan

the section drawing. Cut the top beams (plates) to lap at the corners, and spike them to the posts with 6-inch galvanized nails.

From 4x4s, cut five rafters 6½ feet long and five rafters 4½ feet long. Cut the angles for the rafters and bird's-mouth notches as illustrated on page 57, then nail them to a 2x6 ridgepole and 4x4 plate beams. Then cut and attach two 45-degree 4x4 knee braces to the posts. Use ⅜x4-inch lag screws.

Nail ¾ x 6-inch CCA boards to the sides and back, leaving a 1-inch gap between each board for ventilation.

Cover the ends of the boards with vertical 1x4 trim.

Nail 1x6 fascia trim to the eaves and gable ends.

Roof the shed with hand-split cedar shakes (see pages 31-33).

Build a level platform deck from 2x4 CCA to hold the firewood.

Paint all the CCA lumber with cedar-colored stain.

Figure 5.1—Irish Garden Shed

CHAPTER 5

Irish Garden Shed

❧

I saw this shed while bicycling through the British Isles. Like most things in Europe, it was built to last for centuries. It was probably used to store farming tools. I have taken the liberty of changing the roof, from what was originally thatch, to the more readily available hand-split cedar shakes. You may prefer thatch, board and batten, or even sod (see types of roofing, pages 31-33). Please do not use asphalt shingles; this shed deserves a more elegant roof.

This shed (see Figures 5.1 and 5.2) features timber frame construction, as do several others in this section. Timber framing is one of the traditional construction methods that builders have used for centuries. Building a shed using timbers can be just as easy as conventional stud or "stick framing" (building with 2x4s). A timber-built shed requires fewer pieces, fewer joints and fewer cuts than a stick-built shed, and the end result is often more visually satisfying.

The other outstanding feature of this shed is its log-filled walls. The locust logs take about a day and a half to cut and one week to cement into place, but the materials cost is minimal and the results are spectacular. Locust is among the most rot- and insect-resistant woods growing in the United States. Years ago, houses were built on locust-post foundations, and locust was preferred for fence posts. For your supply, call firewood dealers, landscapers or tree specialists and ask for 12 seasoned 6- to 10-inch-diameter trees cut into 4-foot logs and extra branches, which you will cut into 5-inch sections to fill between the larger logs. If locust is not available, use any other hardwood, sealing the edges with preservative. Make sure the logs are all well seasoned—a radial crack in the log end is a good indication—the crack can be filled while building the wall.

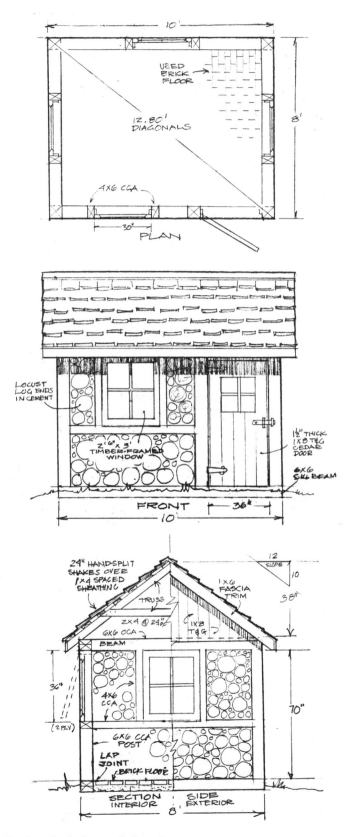

Figure 5.2—Irish Garden Shed plan and elevation

Figure 5.2A

Step-By-Step Instructions
CUTTING THE LOGS

Construct a V-shaped cradle to support the logs while cutting the sections by nailing two 12-inch boards to the sides of a sawhorse as shown in Figure 5.3.

Mark 5 inches from the end of the cradle; this will be your guide to cut each log into 5-inch sections. Place the log in the cradle and using a chain saw, start a cut 5 inches from the end. As you get toward the middle of the cut, take your finger off the trigger so the chain saw blade stops, and keeping the blade in the cut, turn the log over so you can saw through the log without sawing through the cradle. Using this technique, you can whiz through this task safely and with a minimum of fuss (see Figure 5.3).

Figure 5.3—Cutting the logs

GROUNDWORK

Refer to Setting the Offset Stakes, pages 14-15, to prepare the site for this shed. Then dig a trench 24 inches deep and 16 inches wide (see Figure 5.4) and slanted toward the lowest point in the foundation. Run a 4-inch drainage pipe downhill, away from the shed. This will prevent frost heaves from disturbing the shed. Fill the trench with ¾-inch gravel. If you are building in the South, where there is no frost, or in an area where the ground is sandy and percolates well, you can eliminate this step and rest the pressure-treated sill plates directly on the ground. Make sure your timbers are pressure treated, not just dipped, and are rated for ground contact on the end-tag.

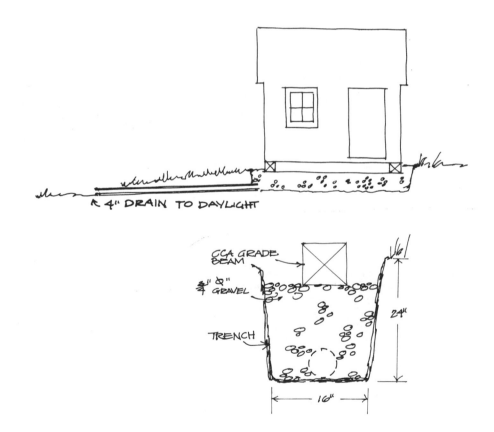

Figure 5.4—Grading and installing drainage

TIMBER FRAMING

The simplest joint used in timber framing is the lap joint, which I recommend using here. Begin by cutting the four foundation 6x6 sill plates to two 8- and 10-foot lengths. Using a circular saw and a square, make several crosscuts halfway through the beam end (see Figure 5.5a). Turn the beam on its side and rip cut (lengthwise) along the bottom of the previous cuts (see Figure 5.5b). Then flip the beam over and repeat the same cut on the opposite side. Turn the beam right side up and chip the pieces out with a mallet and chisel (see Figure 5.5c). Then smooth the surface with a rasp, or better yet, a chain saw, and check for squareness (see Figure 5.5d). Repeat the same four steps on the adjoining beam, and

Figure 5.5—Cutting the lap joint

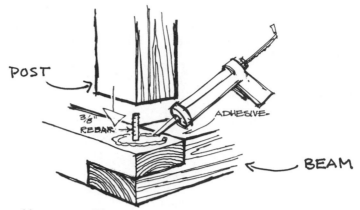

Figure 5.6—Post and beam assembly

nail or pin them together. Repeat with the three other beams. To mark and cut each beam end should take about five minutes.

Next, assemble the beams with their ends overlapping. Take great care to make sure the sill beams rest on well compacted gravel and that they are level. Drill ½-inch holes into the center of the lap joints and place a ⅜-inch rebar in each hole, allowing 3 inches to stick out (see Figure 5.6).

Then cut the four 6x6 corner posts to 70 inches and bore a 3½-inch-deep hole in the bottom center of each corner post. Squeeze some Premium construction adhesive into each hole and drop the posts, one by one, over each corner, fitting the rebar into the holes in the corner posts.

Temporarily nail eight pieces of 1x4 roof nailers (spaced sheathing) securely to the sill plates to prop the posts into position (see Figure 5.7).

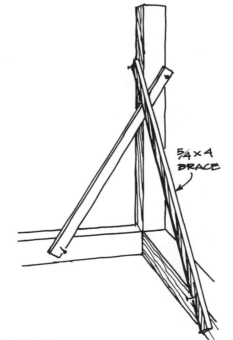

Figure 5.7—Timber framing

BRACING

Make the first corner post absolutely plumb before proceeding to the next corner. When you are finished, double check the diagonal measurement between the top corners. Next, cut the top-plate beams exactly the same as the bottom plate beams and lap the ends the same way. Lean one end of the beam on top of the corner post and push the other end into place (see Figure 5.8). Before installing the top and bottom front timbers, cut a 1-inch-deep notch for the door frame post, 36 inches from the inside of the corner posts. Cut a 6 x 6 to 72 inches to fit the notches (see Figure 5.9).

Figure 5.8—Bracing

Figure 5.9—Notched joint

FRAMELESS WINDOWS

Unlike most, these windows are fitted into the timbers without a frame. Purchase or salvage the windows, and make the timbers fit the windows, rather than the reverse. Begin by hanging the windows (by two 3-inch galvanized butt hinges) from the top beam. Then nail the bottom 4x6 sills and the two 4x6 side window timbers in place. Use a 1/8-inch shim on the sides of the window as a spacer for clearance. Bevel the bottom sill and the window bottom so that the window closes on the beveled sill. Note that the sill must be installed a little higher to allow for the window to fit into the beveled edge. Nail 1x2s to the sides of the frames to act as window stops.

If you want to stain the timber frame, do it before the log walls have been installed in order to avoid spills or drips.

RAFTER TRUSS

Detailed instructions are in Roof Framing and Sheathing on pages 56–59 of the Basic 8x10 Shed. In this case, five trusses are required. Nail two pieces of 6-foot 2x4 together at one end and temporarily place the two legs on the top beams to determine what angles to cut. The gable peak should be about 36 inches high and the rafters should hang out approximately 5 inches beyond the face of the walls. Using a level, mark the plumb angles at the peak and at the point where the rafters touch the top beams. Notch out the rafters to fit the top beams. Cut the peak and the tail ends and join them with a 2x4 collar tie to form a roof truss. Install them at 24-inch centers as shown in the Basic 8x10 Shed figure on page 58.

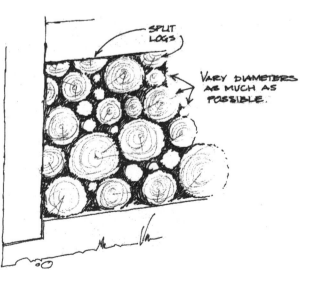

Figure 5.10—Spacing the logs in the walls

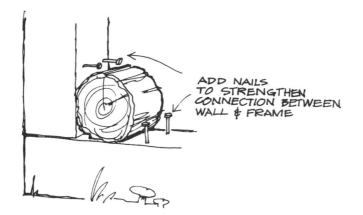

Figure 5.11—Strengthening walls

Figure 5.12—Filling cracks in walls

WALLS

Fill two large garbage pails with sawdust from the local lumberyard, builder or cabinetmaker, and purchase two bags of masonry cement and two bags of lime. Have two cubic yards of sand delivered, and you are ready to begin filling the wall.

In a mortar pail, combine 6 parts sand, 6 parts sawdust, 3 parts Portland cement and 2 parts lime. Measuring accurately is critical.

Gradually add water until the mixture has a plastic feel (not too runny and not too stiff and chunky). The sawdust's function is to make the joints more ductile and allow for shrinkage and expansion of the wood. Lay a thick bed of mortar along the bottom plate, and place the logs side by side on top. Fill the spaces between them with at least ¼ inch of mortar separating the logs at the closest points. If the space between logs is more than 2½ inches, fill in with a small branch section. Split the logs in half, if necessary, where they meet the side posts and vary the log sizes as much as possible to produce an interesting effect (see Figure 5.10). To strengthen the wall, hammer nails between the logs that rest against the timbers (see Figure 5.11). To fill thin cracks, hold a large trowel of mortar upside down, sliding the mortar into the crack with a smaller trowel (see Figure 5.12).

Making a wall with log ends is time-consuming, so allow at least one day per side. After 24 hours, spray the wall with a garden hose and brush off any excess mortar with a wire brush. The mortar mix may take several days to harden.

To finish the walls, fit the gable ends with shiplapped vertical cedar boards, rough side out. Run the tops of the boards above the roof line and trim them off with one pass of the saw as in the 8 x 10 Basic Shed, page 60. Even if you use fairly dry logs, there may be further shrinkage that requires filling.

ROOF

This shed looks best if it is thatched or covered with hand-split cedar shakes (for roof details, see types of roofing, pages 31-33).

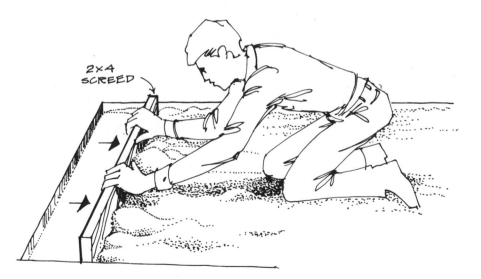

Figure 5.13—Brick floor

FLOOR

When your sand is delivered, also have your masonry supplier deliver 400 used bricks. (This allows 40 extra bricks for waste.) Figure 4½ bricks per square foot of floor. Spread sand inside the shed, leveling it with a 2 x 4 screed. Spray the sand with water, compacting as you work.

Use a straight edge or a long level to lay the bricks (see Figure 5.14). Cut the bricks with a 4-inch chisel and a 4-pound hammer, working over a sand base. Lay the long dimension of the brick perpendicular to the long dimension of the shed. Set the bricks touching each other, then tap them down ¼ inch with a rubber mallet. For a precision job, use string to line up the rows. Uneven rows, however, are more appropriate for a shed and give it a handmade appearance. After laying the brick floor, spread a few shovelfuls of sand over them and sweep the sand into the cracks.

DOOR

Build the door as shown on pages 65-66.

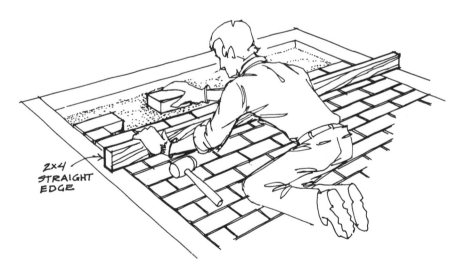

Figure 5.14—Brick floor

Figure 6.1—Japanese Boat Shed

CHAPTER 6

Japanese Boat Shed

The Japanese Boat Shed was built for a couple who love both Japanese design and boats. The long "moon gazing" veranda is a place to contemplate the surrounding gardens. The windowed workshop in the back is convenient for equipment repair. The yearly chore of varnishing and painting the boat is made easier by sliding the five shoji doors open for ventilation and light (see Figures 6.1, 6.2, 6.3).

This shed features square 6x6 pressure-treated poles sunk into the ground every 8 feet. Pole construction is one of the most economical ways to build a large shed, because extensive footings and foundations are eliminated, thus reducing time and materials. Pole construction makes a lot of sense in high-wind or flood areas. Since the poles are embedded in the ground and continue up to the roof, they are unlikely to come out of the ground or bend out of shape. Unlike conventional platform framing, where each floor is a separate layer, poles form an unbroken connection between the ground and the roof.

Pole framing is also recommended for steep or hard-to-reach sites where it is difficult to bring in heavy equipment. Pole framing also allows you to carry all the materials to the site without destroying the soil and vegetation. Although round poles resist bending better than square poles, square poles are more uniform and easier to work with.

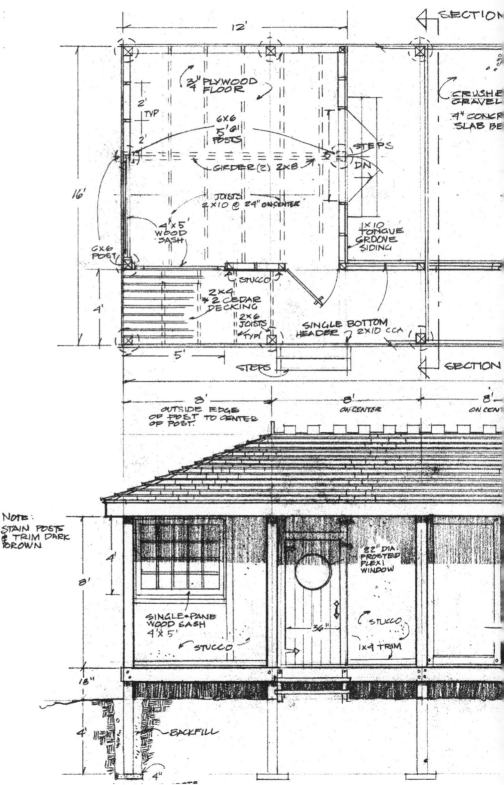

Figure 6.2—Boat shed plans

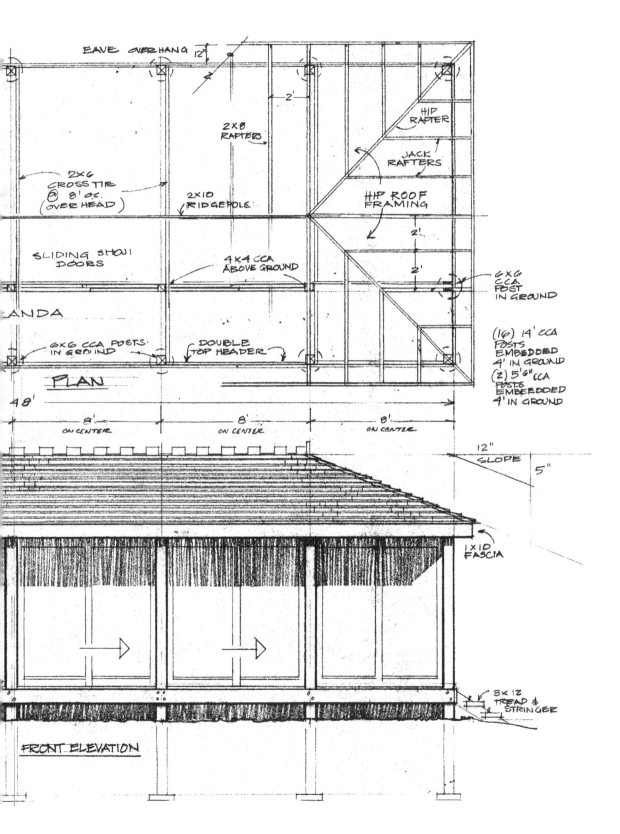

EAVE OVERHANG 12"

2'

2X8 RAFTERS

HIP RAFTER

JACK RAFTERS

2X6 CROSS TIE @ 8' O.C. (OVER HEAD)

2X10 RIDGEPOLE

HIP ROOF FRAMING

2'

SLIDING SHOJI DOORS

4X4 CCA ABOVE GROUND

2'

2'

6X6 CCA POST IN GROUND

ANDA

6X6 CCA POSTS IN GROUND

DOUBLE TOP HEADER

(16) 14' CCA POSTS EMBEDDED 4' IN GROUND

(2) 5'6" CCA POSTS EMBEDDED 4' IN GROUND

PLAN

48'

8' ON CENTER

8' ON CENTER

8' ON CENTER

12" SLOPE

5"

1X10 FASCIA

3X12 TREAD & STRINGER

FRONT ELEVATION

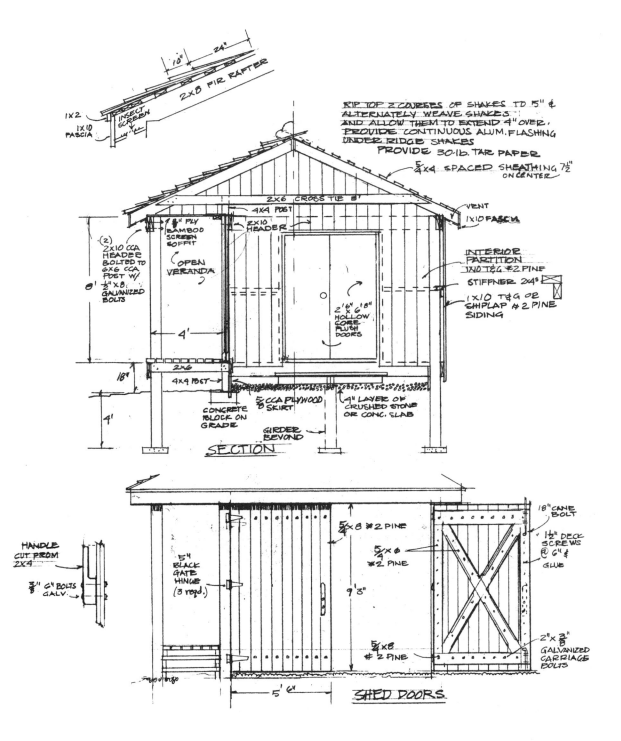

2X8 FIR RAFTER

10" 24"

1X2
INSECT SCREEN
1X10 FASCIA
4"

RIP TOP 2 COURSES OF SHAKES TO 5" &
ALTERNATELY WEAVE SHAKES
AND ALLOW THEM TO EXTEND 4" OVER.
PROVIDE CONTINUOUS ALUM. FLASHING
UNDER RIDGE SHAKES
PROVIDE 30·lb. TAR PAPER
$\frac{5}{4}$X4 SPACED SHEATHING $7\frac{1}{2}$"
ON CENTER

2X6 CROSS TIE 8'
4X4 POST
VENT
1X10 FASCIA

$\frac{1}{8}$" PLY
BAMBOO
SCREEN
SOFFIT
2X10 HEADER

(2)
2X10 CCA
HEADER
BOLTED TO
6X6 CCA
POST W/
$\frac{1}{2}$"X8"
GALVANIZED
BOLTS

8'

OPEN VERANDA

4'

INTERIOR
PARTITION
1X10 T&G #2 PINE
STIFFNER 2X4s
1X10 T&G OR
SHIPLAP #2 PINE
SIDING

2'6"X6'8"
HOLLOW
CORE
FLUSH
DOORS

18"
2X6
4X4 POST

CONCRETE
BLOCK ON
GRADE
$\frac{5}{8}$ CCA PLYWOOD
SKIRT
4" LAYER OF
CRUSHED STONE
OR CONC. SLAB

4'

GIRDER BEYOND

SECTION

HANDLE
CUT FROM
2X4

$\frac{3}{8}$" 6" BOLTS
GALV.

18" CANE
BOLT
1$\frac{1}{2}$" DECK
SCREWS
@ 6" &
GLUE

$\frac{5}{4}$X8 #2 PINE
$\frac{5}{4}$X6
#2 PINE

5"
BLACK
GATE
HINGE
(3 reqd.)

9'3"

$\frac{5}{4}$X8
#2 PINE

2"X $\frac{3}{8}$"
GALVANIZED
CARRIAGE
BOLTS

5' 6"

SHED DOORS

Figure 6.3—Boat shed plans

Step-By-Step Instructions

POLE FRAMING

Begin by laying out the shed as described on pages 14-16. Using the perimeter string, mark the positions of the postholes by driving a short 2 x 2 stake well into the ground. Remember to set the mark inside the perimeter so that the outside face of the post will line up with the string (see Figure 6.4). Use a plumb bob to be sure you are marking exactly vertical.

Dig 18 holes about 4 feet deep and 16 inches in diameter, using a posthole digger or hire the job done. If the ground is particularly hard or rocky, you may need a five-foot pry bar to loosen the material before removing it with the posthole digger. To provide adequate strength to the structure, each post should be embedded a minimum of 4 feet in the ground. Before installing the posts, tamp the soil at the bottom of each hole. You can make your own tamper by boring a hole in an 8-foot 4 x 4 and inserting a 1¼-inch pipe as a handle (see Figure 6.5). For the footings (punch pads), mix and pour two 80-lb. bags of premixed concrete into each hole and allow to set up for several days.

Once you have placed a post in each hole, align the posts by nailing a 16-foot ¾ x 4 temporary brace to a corner post. In order to allow for last-minute adjustments, do not backfill the holes until the main structure has been framed. Measure 8 feet from the outside edge of the corner post, to the center of the next post, and nail the temporary brace in place. Adjust the corner post so it is plumb on both sides and nail two diagonal braces to it, securing them to the ground (see Figure 6.6).

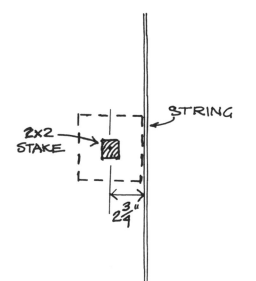

Figure 6.4—Layout

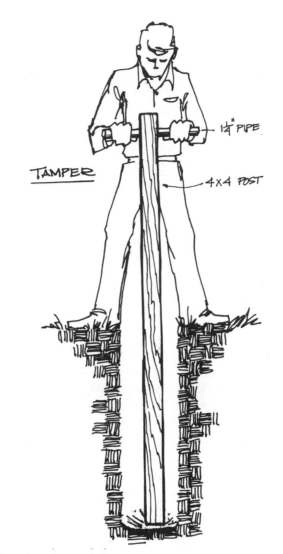

Figure 6.5—Tamping the posthole

Standing on a stepladder, temporarily nail the end of another 16-foot brace near the top of the corner post, using only one nail. Swing the free end up and nail it to the next post (Figure 6.6). Note that the first bay will be slightly narrower, since it was measured from the outside, not the center of the post. Attach temporary supports in the same manner, along both sides of the structure. Check all the diagonals to make sure that the posts are plumb. Add the two diagonal braces to each post once you are sure the post is perfectly aligned. It is helpful to have an assistant hold the post plumb while you nail on the support braces. Nail braces across the two rows of posts in order to connect the two sides together. The frame, at this stage, should look like Figure 6.7.

Snap a level chalk line along the side of the posts, 16½ inches from the ground. Use this mark to bolt the 2 x 10 CCA rim joists to the posts.

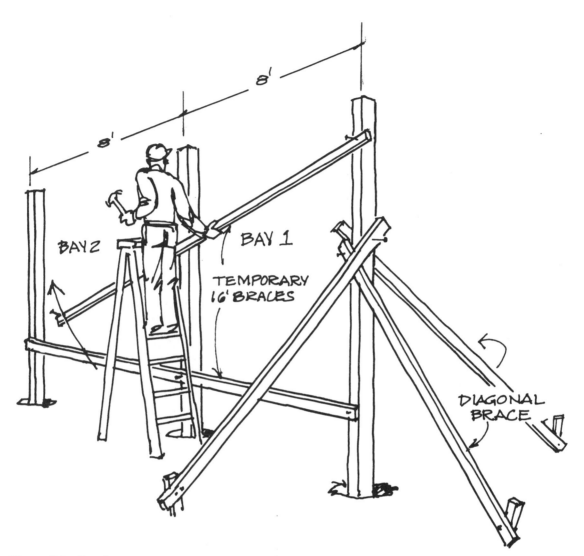

Figure 6.6—Bracing

Use two ½ x 6-inch lag bolts 8 inches at each joint. Snap another chalk line on the posts, 8 feet above the first line, cutting the posts off at this mark. Snap another line 9½ inches below the top of the post, and use this line to cut out a 1½ x 9¼-inch notch for the top 2 x 10 header.

With an assistant, lift the 2 x 10 CCA rim joists up to rest in the notches and bolt them to the posts. Since this upper beam will bear more of the weight than the lower one, another 2 x 10 should be bolted and nailed to it. Use ½ x 8-inch galvanized bolts, 2½-inch common nails and PL 400 adhesive.

Frame the workshop floor by first installing two 2 x 10 girders to the two short center posts. Cut "shoulders" out of the top of the posts, to accept the ends of the girders (see Figure 6.8).

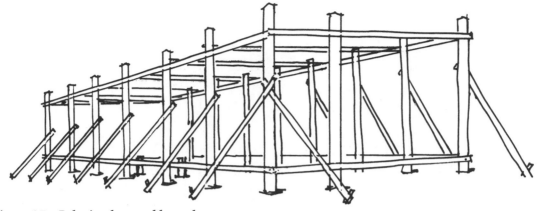

Figure 6.7—Poles in place and braced

HIP ROOF

The hip roof on this shed requires different framing and more building experience than the other sheds in this book. Start by framing the center four bays in the same way as you would frame any gable roof (see Basic 8x10 Shed, pages 56-59). It is important to attach the 2x6 cross ties to the rafters *before* removing the temporary cross braces. The end bays will require slightly longer diagonal corner (hip) rafters. Cut "jack rafters" to meet the hip rafters. If you plan on insulating the workshop, make sure your rafters are a standard 24 inches on center, enabling you to use standard-sized insulation and plasterboard.

SHOJI SLIDING DOORS

For durability, substitute ½-inch Homasote pressed board for the traditional rice paper. Frame the panels in 2x6 and mount them in a track that is formed by the decking and the 2x10 header as detailed in Figure 6.9.

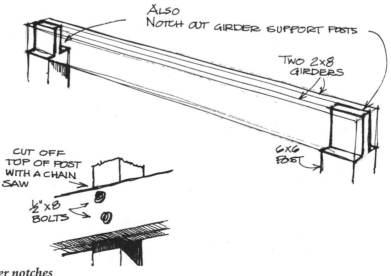

Figure 6.8—Cutting girder notches

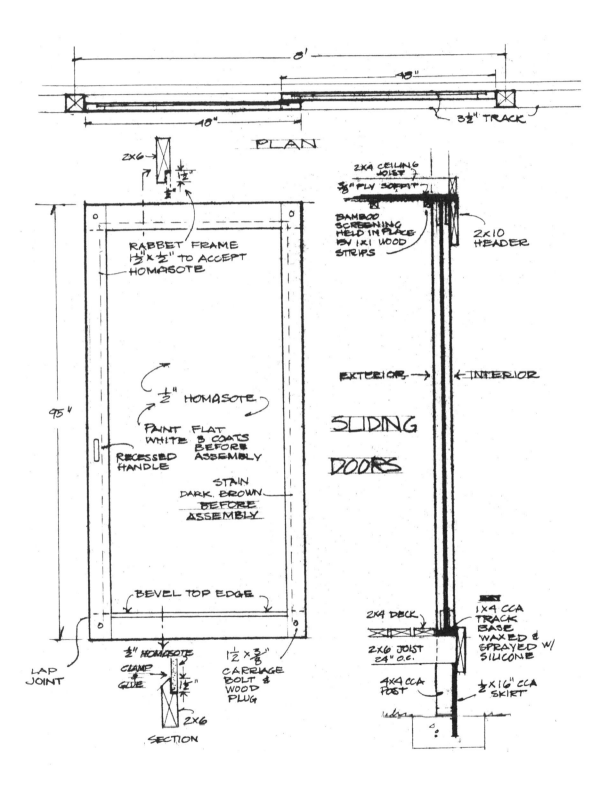

PLAN

8'

48"

18"

3½" TRACK

2×6

1½"

RABBET FRAME
1½" × ½" TO ACCEPT
HOMASOTE

95"

½" HOMASOTE

PAINT FLAT
WHITE 3 COATS
BEFORE
ASSEMBLY

RECESSED
HANDLE

STAIN
DARK BROWN
BEFORE
ASSEMBLY

BEVEL TOP EDGE

LAP
JOINT

½" HOMASOTE

CLAMP
GLUE

1½"

1½ × ⅜"
CARRIAGE
BOLT &
WOOD
PLUG

2×6

SECTION

2×4 CEILING
JOIST

⅜" PLY SOFFIT

BAMBOO
SCREENING
HELD IN PLACE
BY 1×1 WOOD
STRIPS

2×10
HEADER

EXTERIOR →   ← INTERIOR

SLIDING

DOORS

2×4 DECK

2×6 JOIST
24" O.C.

4×4 CCA
POST

1×4 CCA
TRACK
BASE
WAXED &
SPRAYED W/
SILICONE

½ × 16" CCA
SKIRT

Figure 6.9—Shoji sliding doors

Double Doors

The big boat house double doors (see Figure 6.3) are made with ⅝ x 8 #2 tongue-and-groove pine with five 4 x 6 #2 pine cross battens. Using two wide saw horses for support, assemble the tongue-and-groove, and bolt the perimeter battens to the door using ⅜ x 2-inch galvanized bolts and washers. Cut the cross battens so they fit snugly into the corners. Bolt them to the doors. Hang each door on three 5-inch gate hinges and install 18-inch cane bolts on the top and bottom to hold the doors closed.

For attractive handles and latch, cut two L-shapes from 2 x 4s. Allow enough room behind the inside of the handles to hold a 1½-inch-thick cross bar (see plan on page 98).

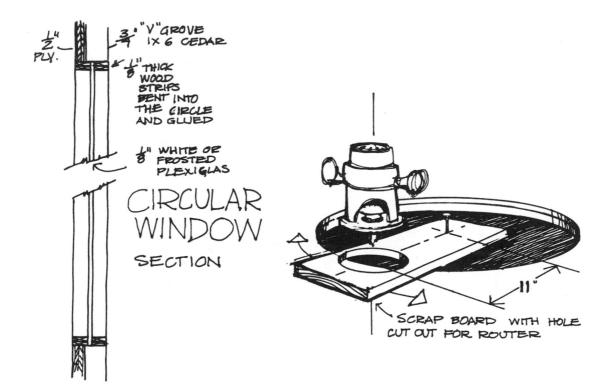

Figure 6.10—Circular window in side door

SIDE DOOR

Build this 36-inch wide door using ½-inch plywood as a backing with ¾-inch tongue-and-groove boards. Glue and screw the plywood to the boards. For the window, cut a 22-inch-diameter hole using a router mounted on a board (and used like a compass) and install a piece of ⅛-inch-thick Plexiglas in the hole. Trim the inside edge with ⅛-inch-thick bent strips of wood (see Figure 6.10). Hang the door with basic ornament hinges.

ORNAMENT

Using an electric jigsaw, cut the decorative roof ornaments from a piece of 2 x 2 using the pattern below and carve the scrolls with a chisel (see Figure 6.11).

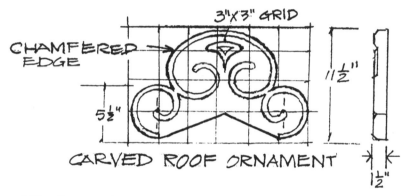

Figure 6.11—Ornament

Figure 7.1—9 x 10 Storage Shed on Posts

CHAPTER 7

9 x 10 Storage Shed on Posts

This project describes how a shed supported by cedar posts buried in the ground can be constructed on a steep hill. When we applied for a building permit for this shed, the inspector found that the intended location was too close to a wetlands area and would require a special natural-resource permit and wetlands setback variance from the local zoning board. Altering the design so that the shed rests on four cedar posts, which have a combined total area of less than 1 square foot, resulted in a structure that posed no threat to the environment or its inhabitants. Ten months later, permission was finally given to start building.

The homeowner wanted a shed for household storage as well as a space where grandchildren could play and sleep when they came to visit. A sleeping loft was a natural solution, a place where kids could unroll their sleeping bags without using up essential storage space. To allow more light and better ventilation, we added two clerestory windows at the top of the shed. In keeping with the architecture of the owner's house, which had an oriental influence, we incorporated sliding doors with a circle motif.

Materials Needed

Quantity	Description	Lengths	Location
Posts, Beams and Floor			
4	4x4 #2 cedar posts	varies	corners
4	2x4 #2 cedar	varies	corners
4	2x6 #2 cedar	varies	corners
2	2x8 #2 fir	8 feet	side floor beams
2	2x8 #2 fir	10 feet	front and rear beams
2	2x6 #2 fir	10 feet	braces
7	2x8 #2 fir	10 feet	joists
12	2x8 joist hangers		joists
3	¾-inch exterior plywood	4 x 8 feet	flooring
Wall Framing			
1	½-inch exterior plywood	4 x 8 feet	header, spacers
14	2x4 #2 fir	8 feet	
18	2x4 #2 fir	10 feet	
4	2x4 #2 fir	12 feet	
4	2x4 #2 fir	14 feet	
3	2x6 #2 fir	10 feet	
4	2x6 #2 fir	8 feet	
Roof Framing			
2	1x6 spruce	10 feet	eaves
30	1x4 spruce	10 feet	space sheathing
7	2x6 #2 fir	10 feet	nailers
12	2x6 joist hangers		rafters
Walls			
4	4x4 #2 cedar posts	varies	corners
52	1x8 rough-sawn shiplapped cedar	10 feet	wall siding
7	1x8 rough-sawn shiplapped cedar	12 feet	wall siding
Windows			
52	1x8 rough-sawn shiplapped cedar	10 feet	wall siding
2	Anderson #41 awning windows		clerestory
2	Anderson #2817 basement awning windows		rear
1	Anderson #AN 41 window		side
Trim			
1	1x8 rough-sawn #2 cedar	12 feet	front fascia
3	1x6 "	12 feet	rear fascia, cap and soffit
1	1x6 "	14 feet	front corners
4	1x4 "	16 feet	side trim
2	1x4 "	10 feet	front trim
2	1x4 "	8 feet	rear trim
1	1x2 "	12 feet	roof trim

QUANTITY	DESCRIPTION	LENGTHS	LOCATION
ROOFING			
5 bundles	18-inch #1 red cedar shingles		
DOORS			
1	sliding door track	8 feet	
2 pairs	hangers with door straps		
3	trolley rail brackets		
1	¾-inch lauan plywood	4 x 8 feet	door
1	½-inch lauan plywood	4 x 8 feet	door
2	1x2 #2 cedar	14 feet	door trim
1 pair	⅛ x 1½-inch lattice	8 feet	circle trim
HARDWARE			
2 tubes	phenoseal caulk		
22 feet	aluminum 12-inch flashing		
3 pieces	10-foot aluminum eave starter strips		
3 lbs.	2-inch shake nails		
3 lbs.	2-inch stainless-steel siding nails		

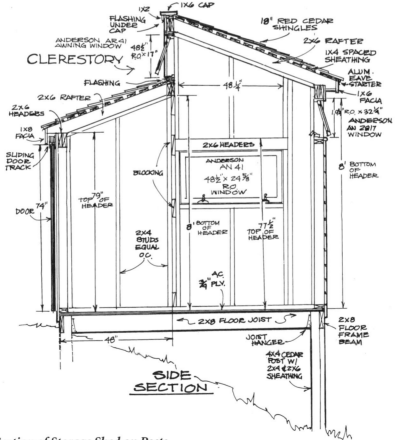

Figure 7.2—Section of Storage Shed on Posts

Posts and Beams

Assuming that your shed will be built on a slope, determine how long the rear post should be by adding the distance between the bottom of the shed and the ground to the distance the post will be embedded in the ground (approximately 30 inches) and the height of the back of the shed (approximately 9 feet). Plan for the posts to be a little long, and cut them off at the top to the exact height after the posts and cross-beams are set.

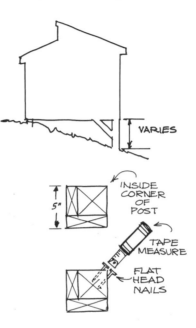

Figure 7.3—Posts

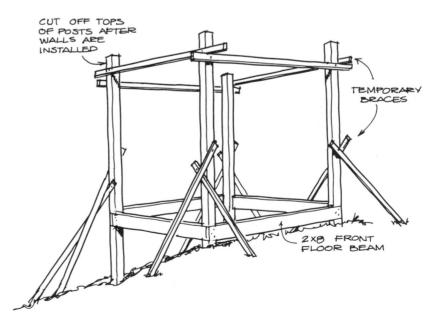

Figure 7.4—Bracing the posts

Lay out the footprint of the shed by measuring and marking a rectangle 16 feet wide by 9 feet deep. Check for squareness by measuring the diagonals and making sure they are equal. Dig four 12-inch-diameter holes to below the frost line, and place a flat rock in each hole to distribute the weight. Nail together one 2x4 and one 2x6 so that they cover two sides of each post, then soak the butt ends in preservative overnight (see Figure 7.3).

Place the front two posts in the uphill holes, and screw a 2x8 front beam at ground level. Temporarily screw the two side 2x8 floor beams to the front post, using only one screw so that it can pivot slightly. Drop in the two rear posts, and screw the two lower side beams to the rear posts. Temporarily clamp the rear floor beam, checking to make sure the posts are all plumb and the beams are level. Make sure the diagonals are equal from corner to corner—hammer two nails to the inside corners of the posts to hold the end of the tape measure.

Temporarily screw the 2x3s to the top of the posts (you'll need a stepladder). After making sure all the posts are square and plumb, attach two temporary 1x4 braces to all the posts (see Figure 7.4). Keep these braces in place as long as possible, as they will keep the rest of your construction from getting out of line.

After clearly marking each of the floor beams, remove them one at a time, and cut out notches where they join the posts (see Figure 7.5). Screw the end of each floor beam to the posts with three 3½-inch galvanized screws.

Figure 7.5—Cut out notches

KNEE BRACES

Cut four 5-foot 2x6 knee braces, and attach them to the rear posts to make the structure rigid. Cut the brace ends at a 45-degree angle. Mark and "let in" the ends of the braces by cutting out notches using an electric jigsaw and a chisel (see Figure 7.6).

FLOOR

To support the ¾-inch plywood floor, cut and install six 2x8 fir floor joists, using 2x8 metal joist hangers to connect the ends to the floor beams, placing them 16 inches on center. Add 2x8 cross-blocking between the floor joists where the 4 x 8-foot plywood panels end. Using 2½-inch (8d) nails, nail the first two sheets of plywood every 8 inches. Cut a third sheet of plywood (see Figure 7.7) into three pieces to fill in the remaining areas. Notch out the corners to accept the posts.

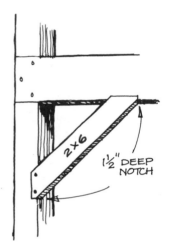

Figure 7.6—Knee brace

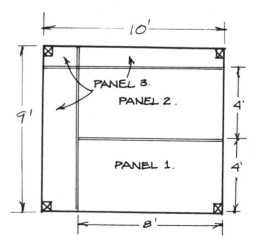

Figure 7.7—Floor panels

WALL FRAMING

Frame the walls with 2x4s, starting with the rear wall. Build the walls using the floor as a work platform, and tilt the wall frames up into place, nailing them to the posts. Use double 2x6 headers over the windows and doors, with ½-inch plywood spacers between the headers to bring their combined width to 3½ inches. Make sure you allow the specified rough opening (RO) for the windows. The manufacturer generally allows a small clearance for adjustments. To play it safe, buy the windows first, check their actual measurements before beginning and make adjustments if necessary. Install two sets of 2x6 headers across the interior where the two roofs meet (see Figure 7.8).

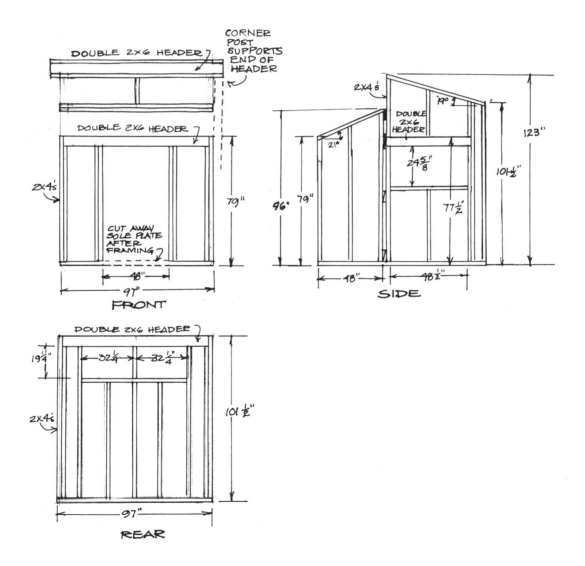

Figure 7.8—Wall framing

ROOF FRAMING

Install seven 2x6 roof rafters, spaced equidistantly, on both roofs with 2x6 metal hangers. Cut the ends of the rafters as shown below. Make sure the tail ends line up by attaching a string that joins the outside rafters. Cut off the tops of the corner posts. Cover the rafters with 1 x 4 spaced sheathing (nailers), except for the first board, which is a 1x6 and overlaps the ends of the rafters by 1 inch. The second board (a 1x4) is butted up to the 1x6. The remaining 1x4 nailers are spaced 2 inches apart. Make sure there is no gap in the sheathing at the top (see Figure 7.10).

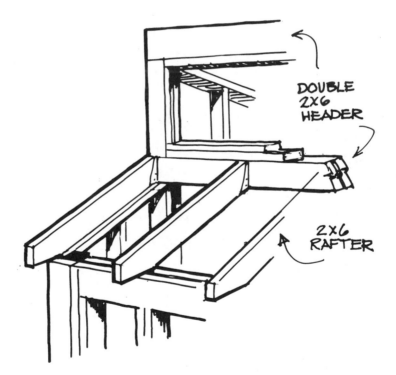

Figure 7.9—Rafters

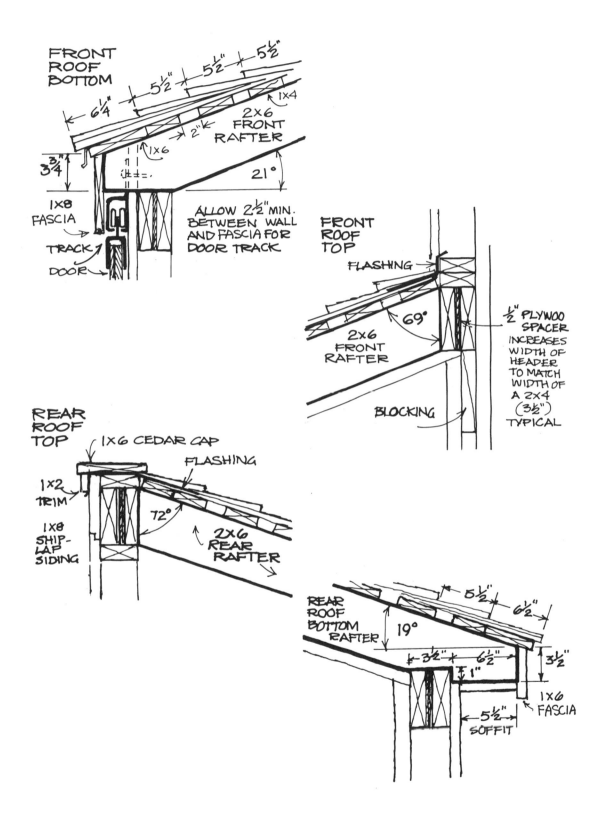

FRONT ROOF BOTTOM

$6\frac{1}{4}"$ $5\frac{1}{2}"$ $5\frac{1}{2}"$ $5\frac{1}{2}"$ $5\frac{1}{2}"$

1×4

2×6 FRONT RAFTER

2"

1×6

$3\frac{3}{4}"$

21°

1×8 FASCIA

TRACK

DOOR

ALLOW $2\frac{1}{2}"$ MIN. BETWEEN WALL AND FASCIA FOR DOOR TRACK

FRONT ROOF TOP

FLASHING

69°

2×6 FRONT RAFTER

BLOCKING

$\frac{1}{2}"$ PLYWOO SPACER INCREASES WIDTH OF HEADER TO MATCH WIDTH OF A 2×4 ($3\frac{1}{2}"$) TYPICAL

REAR ROOF TOP

1×6 CEDAR CAP

FLASHING

1×2 TRIM

1×8 SHIP-LAP SIDING

72°

2×6 REAR RAFTER

REAR ROOF BOTTOM RAFTER

$5\frac{1}{2}"$ $6\frac{1}{2}"$

19°

$3\frac{1}{2}"$ $6\frac{1}{2}"$

$3\frac{1}{2}$

1"

1×6 FASCIA

$5\frac{1}{2}"$

SOFFIT

Figure 7.10—Roof-framing details

SHEATHING AND TRIM

Install the windows by nailing the vinyl flanges onto the rough opening studs before covering the walls. Sheathe the shed walls with horizontal 1x8 rough-sawn shiplapped boards, and cover the ends of the boards with 1x4 cedar trim (see Figure 7.11). Do not attach the 1x8 front fascia until the doors are hung. Nail the 1x6 soffit underneath the ends of the rear rafters, and nail the rear 1x6 fascia to the rafter ends.

ROOFING

Install the brown aluminum eave starter strips at the bottom edge of the roofs, and nail on 18-inch red cedar shingles with 5½ inches exposure. Use a 1x6 board as a straightedge to line up the bottom of the shingles as you proceed up the roof. Be sure to cut and install the 1x4 wall and fascia trim before shingling, allowing the shingles to overlap the trim pieces by ½ inch. Add a 12-inch-wide strip of aluminum flashing at the top of the front roof before adding the sheathing to the clerestory. Cap the top edge of the rear roof with aluminum flashing and 1x6 and 1x2 trim.

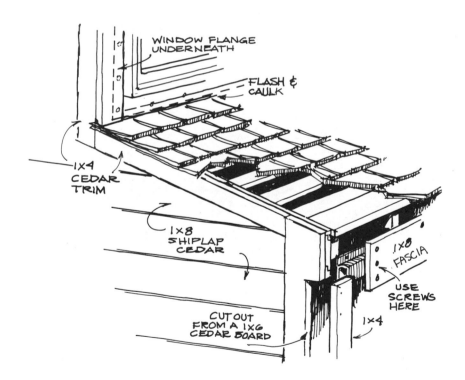

Figure 7.11—Trim

Doors

The two sliding doors are made by making a sandwich of ¾- and ½-inch lauan plywood. Cut a 36-inch-diameter circle out of the ½-inch lauan plywood, then cut both the ½- and ¾-inch pieces of plywood in half. Cut all the panels to 6-foot lengths, and glue them to each other. To make the circle stand out, stain it with a light walnut stain.

Protect the vertical side edges of the doors by cutting four pieces of 1x2 and rabbeting out a 1¼-inch shoulder to fit the door. To trim the circle, cut two pieces of wood, ³⁄₁₆ inch x 1 inch x 10 feet, put glue on them, and bend them into the inside edge of the circle (see Figure 7.12).

Give the lauan plywood two coats of an oil-base sealer such as CWF, and hang them from a box rail and hanger system sold for heavy-duty sliding doors. Follow accompanying instructions. Once the doors are hung, screw the front fascia on to cover the track, and you are finished.

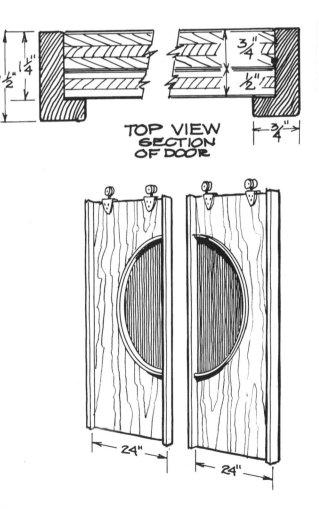

Figure 7.12—Doors

SKYLIGHT

STORAGE

REAR VIEW

Figure 8A—10 x 11 Potting Shed

CHAPTER 8

More Special-Use Sheds

❧

10 x 11 Potting Shed

Ask a dozen shed owners what they keep in their sheds, and you will probably get a different answer from each. But a shed doesn't have to be a catchall for storing extra household items. It can have a special use and provide a pleasant space in which to work on hobbies such as gardening, woodworking or even painting or sculpting.

A perfect size for a potting shed, this 10 x 11 shed has a shape that is typical of many barns found in the northeastern United States, where farmers started with a simple gable-roofed structure and later added a shed roof off the back. The shed features a skylight, which floods the interior space with light (a feature lacking in most sheds), and an overhang in the rear where you can store bikes, firewood or lawn equipment. The proportions are ideal—it's big enough to store all the necessary garden tools, potting soil and plant containers and still provide ample room in which to work. The shed is essentially a timber-frame version of the Basic 8 x 10 Shed (see Irish Garden Shed, pages 87-88). Directions specify cedar timber framing with simple lap joints; however, they can easily be adapted for 2x4 construction.

The workbench is a simplified version of the one shown on page 133. If the windows are salvaged from old houses, make sure they are the same size. If old windows are not available, then single-sash barn windows, as shown in the section view of the plans, can be special-ordered from your lumberyard. The walls in the plans are built with 1x8 shiplapped #2 cedar, but any siding, including board and batten, can be used. Similarly, any roofing material can be used.

Materials Needed

Quantity	Description	Lengths	Location
Floor Framing			
3	2x6 PT lumber	10 feet	front & back frame and blocking
2	2x6 PT lumber	12 feet	floor frame (sides)
4	2x6 PT lumber	12 feet	floor joists @ 24 inches on center
3	¾-inch exterior plywood	4 x 8 feet	flooring
6	concrete half-blocks	4 x 8 x 16 inches	foundation (additional blocks may be required, depending on site)
Wall Framing			
6	4x4 #2 cedar	6 feet	4 corner and 2 door posts
2	4x4 #2 cedar	5 feet	rear corner posts
2	4x4 #2 cedar	10 feet	knee braces
3	4x6 #2 cedar	10 feet	front, middle and rear beams
2	4x6 #2 cedar	8 feet	side beams
6	⁵⁄₄ x 6 PT decking	10 feet	rear deck
12	spikes	6 inches	beam lap joints
16	⅜-inch lag screws	5 inches	knee braces
10	2x4 #2 cedar	6 feet	wall studs
1	2x4 #2 cedar	8 feet	rough sills
Roof Framing			
12	2x4 #2 const. fir	6 feet	rafters
6	2x4 #2 const. fir	5 feet	collar ties
6	2x4 #2 const. fir	4 feet	rear rafters
Siding			
24	1x8 shiplapped #2 cedar	10 feet	front and rear walls
24	1x8 #2 cedar	12 feet	sides
3 lbs.	2-inch galvanized siding nails		
Skylight			
2	2x4 clear cedar	6 feet	skylight curb
2	2x4 clear cedar	4 feet	skylight curb
2	1x2 #2 pine	4 feet	side ledges
1	Plexiglas	48 x 73½ x ¼ inches	skylight
1	⅛ x ½-inch glazier's tape	30 feet	skylight
1	2 x 2-inch aluminum angle bar	73½ inches	skylight top
2	2 x 2-inch aluminum angle bar	48 inches	skylight sides

Quantity	Description	Lengths	Location
Trim			
2	1x4 #2 cedar	12 feet	ridge trim
2	1x4 #2 cedar	12 feet	front and rear fascia
2	1x2 #2 cedar	12 feet	front and rear fascia trim
2	1x4 #2 cedar	14 feet	gable trim
2	1x2 #2 cedar	14 feet	gable trim
2	2¾-inch #2 cedar	71 inches	door casing
1	2x4 PT lumber	38 inches	pent above door
6	2¼-inch #2 cedar	36 inches	window-jamb casing
3	2¼-inch #2 cedar	30 inches	casing above window
4	1x4 #2 cedar	7 feet	front corner boards
4	1x4 #2 cedar	5 feet	rear corner boards
1 roll	insect screen 6 inches wide		eaves
2	1x2 #2 pine	12 feet	trim for eaves
Finished Roofing			
2	1x8 #2 pine	12 feet	roof eaves
17	1x4 #2 pine	12 feet	roof
7 bundles	#1 red cedar shingles	18 inches	roof
6 lbs.	galvanized roofing nails	3d	roof
1 roll	aluminum	8 inches wide	flashing
2	1x4 #2 cedar	12 feet	ridge
Door			
5	1x8 #2 shiplapped cedar	6 feet	door
1	⁵⁄₄x8 #2 pine	6 feet	battens
1	⁵⁄₄x4 #2 pine	6 feet	brace
24	#10 flathead wood screws	1⅜ inches	
2	strap hinges	10 inches long	
1	1⅛-inch-diameter wood dowel	8 inches	latch
1	2x4 pine	12 inches	latch
1	1x2 pine	12 inches	latch
Windows			
3	2x3 clear cedar	10 feet	window rails and stiles
3	1x6 #2 cedar	10 feet	window frames and muntins
3	Plexiglas	⅛ x 20 x 29 inches	window panes
1 tube	clear silicone caulk	-	bedding for Plexiglas
3	window catches	-	windows
3	screw eyes	½ inch	windows
3	⅛-inch-diameter nylon cord	24 inches	windows

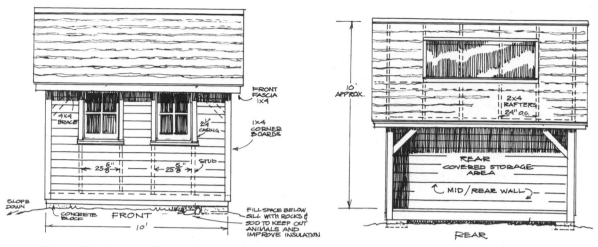

Figure 8B—Front and rear views

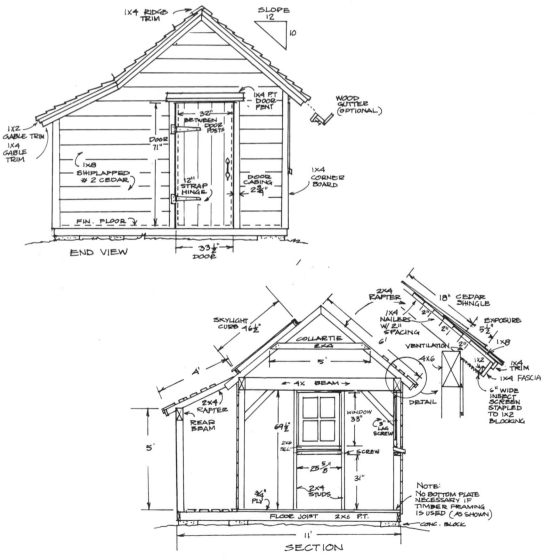

Figure 8C—End of section views

Step-By-Step Instructions

FLOOR FRAMING

Clear a flat surface, and measure and mark the space on which your shed will be built. The floor frame will be supported by concrete blocks under each corner. This allows you the option of moving the shed at a later date if necessary. Cut six pieces of 2x6, each 10 feet 9 inches long (two for the perimeter frame and four for the floor joists). Make the floor frame by nailing two pieces of 10-foot lumber to two pieces of 10-foot 9-inch lumber, attaching them so that the rear and front pieces of the frame overlap the two side pieces.

Position the floor frame on top of the concrete blocks. Square the floor frame so that the diagonals measure 14.86 feet (178⅜ inches). Make sure that it is level. Adjust the concrete blocks with shims if necessary. Install four floor joists at 2-foot intervals. Cut and toenail 2x6 "blocking" between floor joists. Nail down 2½ sheets of plywood using 6d nails every 8 inches (see Figure 8D).

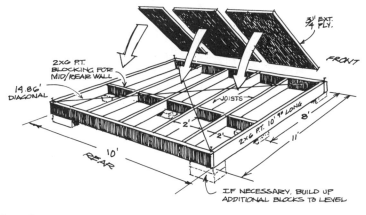

Figure 8D—Floor frame

WALL FRAMING

Cut four 4x4 corner posts 69½ inches long and two 4x4 rear posts 56 inches long. Use 1x2s to temporarily prop up the posts while toenailing them to the floor. Cut three 10-foot beams and two 8-foot beams. Notch the beam ends to form lap joints. Position 10-foot beams on the tops of the posts, and nail a 6-inch spike through the beams and into each corner post.

Fit shorter beams into the notches provided in the 10-foot beams, and "spike" again. Cut 10 2-foot knee braces. Miter-cut ends at a 45-degree angle. Install braces at each corner using ⅜ x 5-inch lag screws (see Detail in Figure 8E).

Install 4x4 posts for the door frame. The distance between doorway posts should measure 32 inches. Cut 10 2x4 studs, each 69½ inches long.

Install window studs, spaced 25⅝ inches apart. Install interior wall studs, spaced approximately 24 inches on center. Install rough sills using screws (to allow for adjustments). Check for plumb (see Figure 8E).

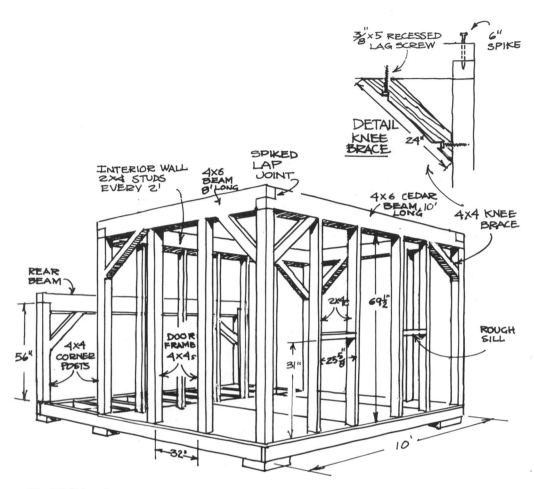

Figure 8E—Wall framing

SIDING

The walls are covered with 1x8 shiplapped boards. We recommend using rough-sawn cedar, which is rot-resistant and weathers to a soft gray. Start installing the siding at the bottom of each wall using 2-inch galvanized siding nails. To prevent rain from entering the shed, make sure that each successive board overlaps the one below.

ROOF FRAMING

Cut twelve 6-foot rafters, and cut the tops at a 40-degree angle. Using the shed floor as a work platform, lay two rafters down flat, and join the tops using 2½-inch screws.

To mark the location of the bird's mouth, temporarily lay an 8-foot 2x4 (which represents the width of the shed) approximately 6 inches up from the bottom end of each rafter, and mark with a pencil. Cut six 5-foot 2x4 collar ties. Cut the ends off at a 40-degree angle. Screw them to the rafters, making sure the ends do not protrude past the outer edge of the rafters, as this would interfere with roofing. Cut bird's-mouth notches, and screw each pair of rafters to the top beam. Use a 1x4 to

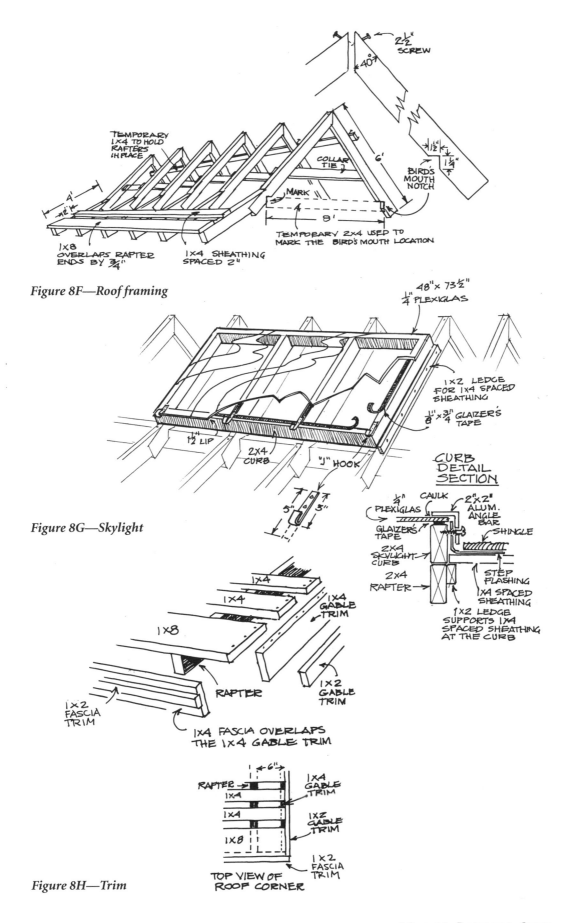

2½" SCREW

40°

1½"
1¼"

BIRD'S MOUTH NOTCH

6'

COLLAR TIE

MARK

8'

TEMPORARY 2X4 USED TO MARK THE BIRD'S MOUTH LOCATION

TEMPORARY 1X4 TO HOLD RAFTERS IN PLACE

4'

1½"

1X8 OVERLAPS RAFTER ENDS BY 3¾"

1X4 SHEATHING SPACED 2"

Figure 8F—Roof framing

48" × 73½"
¼" PLEXIGLAS

1X2 LEDGE FOR 1X4 SPACED SHEATHING

⅛" × ¾" GLAIZER'S TAPE

1½ LIP

2X4 CURB

"J" HOOK

5"
5"

Figure 8G—Skylight

CURB DETAIL SECTION

CAULK
2"× 2" ALUM. ANGLE BAR
¼" PLEXIGLAS
GLAIZER'S TAPE
SHINGLE
2X4 SKYLIGHT CURB
2X4 RAFTER
STEP FLASHING
1X4 SPACED SHEATHING
1X2 LEDGE SUPPORTS 1X4 SPACED SHEATHING AT THE CURB

1X4
1X4
1X8

1X4 GABLE TRIM

1X2 GABLE TRIM

RAFTER

1X2 FASCIA TRIM

1X4 FASCIA OVERLAPS THE 1X4 GABLE TRIM

6"

RAFTER
1X4
1X4
1X8

1X4 GABLE TRIM

1X2 GABLE TRIM

1X2 FASCIA TRIM

TOP VIEW OF ROOF CORNER

Figure 8H—Trim

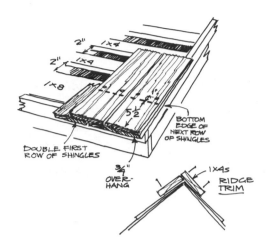

Figure 8I—Roof

temporarily hold the rafters in place. Cut six 4-foot rafters for the rear addition. Hold the end of one 4-foot 2x4 up to an existing rafter end and rear beam, and mark where the next bird's mouth and rafter joint should go. Cut out the notches, and screw them in place with 3-inch galvanized deck screws. To provide a base for the cedar shingles, nail a 1x8 to the bottom of the rafters, overlapping the bottom edge of the rafters by ¾ inch. The remaining 1x4s are spaced 2 inches apart (see Figure 8F).

SKYLIGHT

The feature that sets this shed apart from the others in this book is the 4 x 6-foot skylight (see Figure 8G). Build a 46½ x 73½-inch "curb" out of 2x4s, and screw it directly over the existing rafters. Note that headers are not necessary here because rafters remain intact. Bend over four ½ x 5-inch metal straps to form J-hooks, and screw them to the bottom of the curb to hold the bottom edge of the Plexiglas.

Lay ½ x ⅛-inch glazier's tape over the top edge of the skylight curb.

Carefully lay a 48 x 73½-inch piece of ¼-inch Plexiglas on top of the glazier's tape. The Plexiglas and the J-hooks holding it should overhang the curb by 1 inch to allow for water runoff. After the skylight is installed, continue shingling the roof, making sure to use stepped flashing where shingles meet the skylight curb. Once shingling is finished, complete the skylight by screwing a 2 x 2 x ⅛-inch aluminum angle bar to the sides and top (see Figure 8G).

TRIM AND ROOFING

Trim the two gable roof ends with 1x4 cedar. Nail the ends of the spaced sheathing to the top of the gable trim. Add the front and rear 1x4 fascias, the 1x2 gable trim and the 1x2 fascia trim in that order. Cover the four corners with two 1x4s nailed to each other and to the walls (see Figure 8H).

Cover the 1x4 spaced sheathing with 18-inch cedar shingles. Use

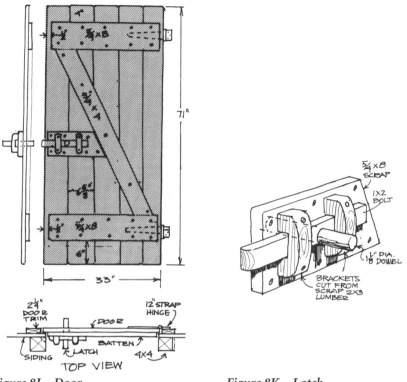

Figure 8J—Door   Figure 8K—Latch

1-inch galvanized roofing nails. Double the first row of shingles, and overhang the edge of the roof by ¾ inch. Stagger each row so that the seams do not line up. Make each row 5½ inches above the previous one, using a 1x6 board as a guide on which to rest the bottom of the shingles before nailing them (see Figure 8I). Cap off the ridge with two 1x4 beveled boards, caulked and nailed together.

Door

On a flat surface, place side by side five pieces of 6-foot 1x8 shiplapped cedar. Saw off the edges on the two end pieces so that the door measures 32 inches wide. Cut two pieces of ⁵⁄₄ x 8, each 31 inches long, and one piece of 5-foot-long ⁵⁄₄ x 4. Screw the two battens to the door. Mark and cut a ⁵⁄₄ x 4 diagonal brace to fit diagonally between the top batten and the hinged side of the bottom batten. Screw two 10-inch strap hinges to the front of the door (see Figure 8J).

To hang the door, screw the other half of the hinges to a piece of 2¼-inch cedar door trim. Hold the door in place, and allowing for a ³⁄₁₆-inch clearance, nail the trim and the door to the shed. Add the 38-inch pent roof and the 2¼-inch casing to the top of the door.

A wooden latch can be made from a piece of 1x2, two pieces of 2x3 and an ⅛-inch diagonal dowel (see Figure 8K). Cut a 1¼ x 3-inch slot in the door for the dowel to extend to the exterior. Mount the latch on a piece of ⁵⁄₄ x 8, and screw it to the inside of the door.

WINDOWS

You can special-order the three 24 x 33-inch windows from your local lumberyard for about $75 each, or you can build them yourself for less than $10 each. Each window requires:

    1 2x3, 10 feet long (choose very straight wood)
    1 piece of ⅛-inch-thick Plexiglas, 20 x 29 inches
    2-inch screws

For each window, cut two 33-inch pieces of 2x3 lumber for the "stiles" and two 22-inch pieces of 2x3 for the "rails."

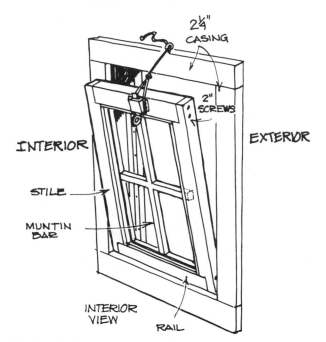

Figure 8L—Tilt-in window

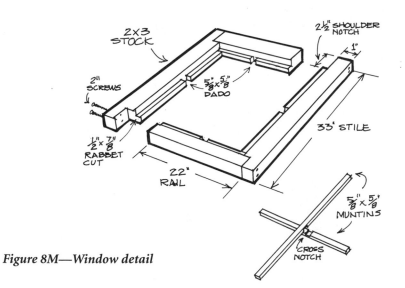

Figure 8M—Window detail

Using a table saw, make a $^7/_8$ x ½-inch rabbet cut into one edge of each 2x3 (see Figure 8M). Cut a 2½-inch shoulder notch in each end of the 33-inch 2x3s. Make a ⅝-inch-wide, ⅝-inch-deep dado cut in the middle of each 2x3 to accept the muntins, which will be put on later.

Glue and screw the sash together, using 2-inch screws. Lay a bead of clear silicone in the rabbeted groove provided in the window, and insert the Plexiglas panel into the groove. Use brads to nail waste strips (left over from cutting the rabbets) over the edges of the Plexiglas to hold it in place. Cut and glue ⅝ x ⅝-inch muntin strips to the front of the window. Install a window catch to the top of the window.

To Hang the Window

Build a 4¾-inch-wide window frame to fit inside the rough opening, allowing ⅛-inch clearance between the window and the frame. Measure and cut the sill from a piece of pressure-treated 2x6, 30⅝ inches long, beveling the front and back edges at a 15-degree angle. It should extend ¼ inch past the outside edges of the 2¼-inch casing. Install the sill over the 2 x 4-foot rough opening. Cut the bottom ends of the two window casings at 15 degrees to fit the sill, and nail them in place. Frame the inside and outside of the window opening with 2¼-inch casing. Mortise a small hole for the window catch bolt, and install a cord to hold the window open. To keep the window in place, cut and nail ¾ x ¾-inch stops to the side window frames, as shown in Figure 8N. Open the window by releasing the catch and tilting it back. No rain will get in, and the window can be easily removed for maintenance.

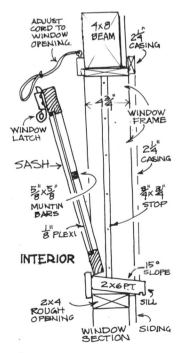

Figure 8N—Window section

Figure 8.5—Work Shed

Work Shed

This is a workshop that even Norm Abrams of "This Old House" would be proud of. Just look at the features: good ventilation, high ceilings, lots of drawers, shelves and electrical outlets, wall space for hanging tools, and storage for lumber. It has doors on both ends, so long boards can be rip cut without hitting the wall and there is natural light from the clerestory windows above.

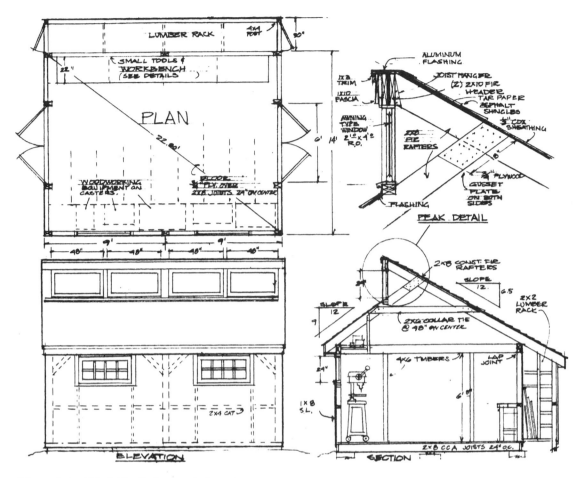

Figure 8.6—Work Shed plan and elevation

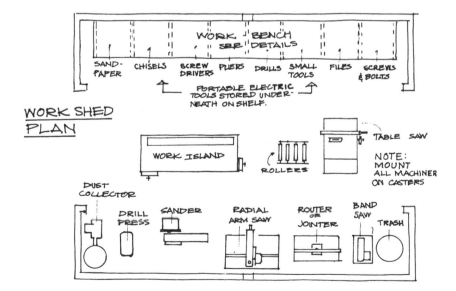

WORK SHED
PLAN

Figure 8.7—Work Shed floor plan

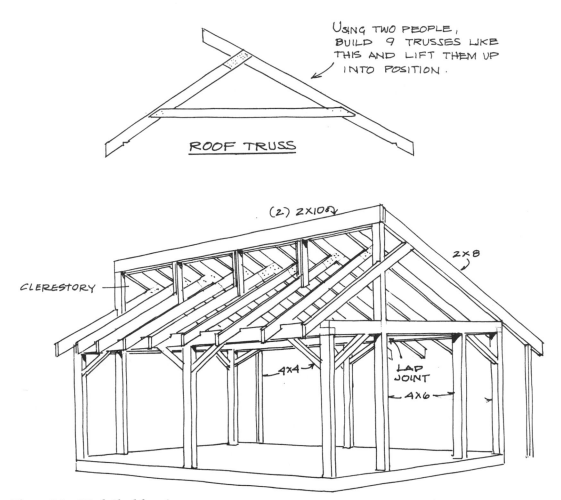

USING TWO PEOPLE, BUILD 9 TRUSSES LIKE THIS AND LIFT THEM UP INTO POSITION.

ROOF TRUSS

(2) 2X10

CLERESTORY

2X8

4X4

LAP JOINT

4X6

Figure 8.8—Work Shed framing

Start with a solid, level floor, either a poured concrete slab or a simple box frame platform similar to that of the Basic 8 x 10 Shed, pages 53-55.

Timber-frame this shed, using simple lap joints and knee braces (see Irish Garden Shed, pages 87-88). Rough cedar timbers are lighter and look nice, but any construction fir will do. The rafters are butt-jointed near the peak with ½-inch-thick plywood gusset plates (see Figure 8.8). The header at the peak (or ridge) is a combination of two pieces of 2 x 10 fir, 18 feet long, with a piece of ½-inch-thick plywood sandwiched between them. Build the trusses first and build the header in place. You should have an assistant and safe scaffolding to build this part of the shed.

Cover the roof with ½-inch CDX plywood and shingle it with asphalt shingles as directed on pages 63-64. Buy six 4 x 2-foot rough-opening, awning-type windows. Install two in the lower front wall and four in the clerestory. The two lower windows (sometimes called "stable windows") look nicer divided into eight panes; however, this does increase the cost.

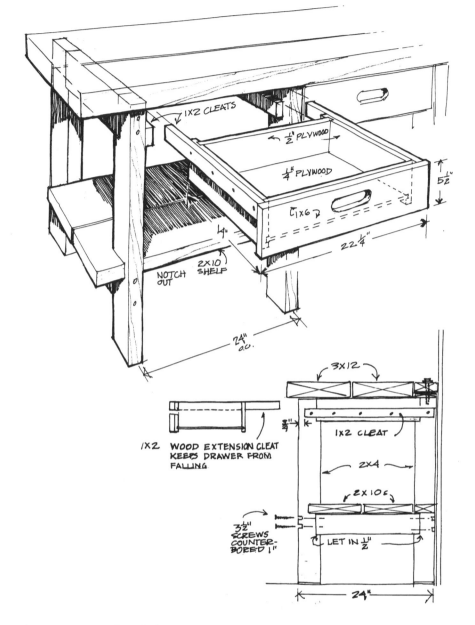

Figure 8.9—Workbench details

Install 2x4 cats around the outside walls and cover the walls with 1x8 shiplapped northern pine. Build the doors out of ⅝-inch exterior plywood braced with ¾ x 6 battens. Use the leftover 2-foot-wide plywood for the doors in the lumber storage area. Build the lumber racks out of 2x2s, making sure to provide an area for large sheets of material.

Build the workbench of 2x4s for frames and 3x12s for the top. Make drawers out of 1x6s and ¼-inch plywood. Attach 1x2 "cleats" (see Figure 8.9) to act as extensions, so that the drawer won't drop if it is pulled out too far.

Figure 8.10—Victorian Shed

Victorian Shed

This structure can be used as a children's playhouse or a backyard gazebo (see Figures 8.10, 8.11). Use as much molding as you like and paint the entire structure white, so that the details stand out. This is an excellent project for anyone who enjoys cutting and fitting small decorative parts together. This shed took a month to build. It requires advanced woodworking skills and the ability to build from the illustrations. Only highlights of construction are included here. It might be more convenient to build this one in your garage or workshop for easy access to tools and move it to the site later. It requires a simple ¾-inch CCA plywood floor, nailed to a 2x4 CCA base.

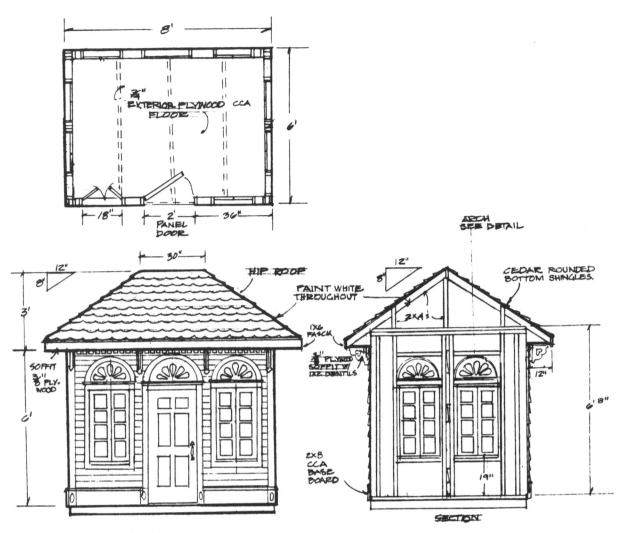

Figure 8.11—Victorian Shed plan and elevation

Frame the shed with 2x4s (see Figure 8.12), keeping the two angles of the hip roof the same. Make sure the tail ends of the rafters line up with each other.

Form the 18-inch radius over the windows, using ¾ x 3½-inch wide exterior plywood with "kerf" cuts made in the back and bent into an arch (see Figure 8.13). Using a beam compass, draw the curved 2½-inch-wide, 18-inch radius window trim onto a ⅛-inch board and cut it out with an electric jigsaw. Also, cut out the fan windows from ¾-inch solid core plywood (18¾-inch radius) and carefully cut the flower-petal shapes out with a jigsaw or scroll saw. You will need 18 pieces of ¾-inch exterior plywood cut to 9x32 inches for the casement windows. Cut the window panes and mold the edges of the opening in the window and the fan window with a router bit (see Figure 8.13). Fill any voids with vinyl spackling compound, and sand, prime and install them with hinges. Cover the walls with clear cedar

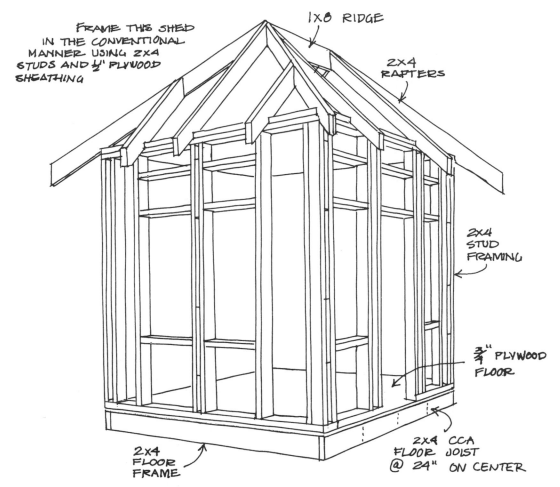

FRAME THIS SHED IN THE CONVENTIONAL MANNER USING 2X4 STUDS AND ½" PLYWOOD SHEATHING

1X8 RIDGE

2X4 RAFTERS

2X4 STUD FRAMING

¾" PLYWOOD FLOOR

2X4 FLOOR FRAME

2X4 CCA FLOOR JOIST @ 24" ON CENTER

Figure 8.12—Victorian Shed framing

5-inch-wide clapboard, leaving a 3-inch exposure. At the eaves, install a 3-inch trim board. Glue and nail 1½-inch-wide dentils onto the trim board.

Add decorative ornaments wherever possible in order to give the shed a gingerbread appearance. You can buy decorative moldings, but it is less expensive to make your own originals. The decorative brackets, for instance, can be cut from ¾-inch solid-core plywood attached to 1 x 3 L-shaped backs and installed under the eaves.

Cover the roof with specially ordered round-bottomed cedar shingles, or make your own by cutting long strips of ¼ x 12-inch plywood and scalloping the bottom edge with a jigsaw.

The 2 x 4-foot optional front door is made from two sheets of ¾-inch exterior plywood. Cut rectangular holes for the panels, and glue and screw the two pieces together.

Paint the entire shed inside and out with three coats of semigloss enamel.

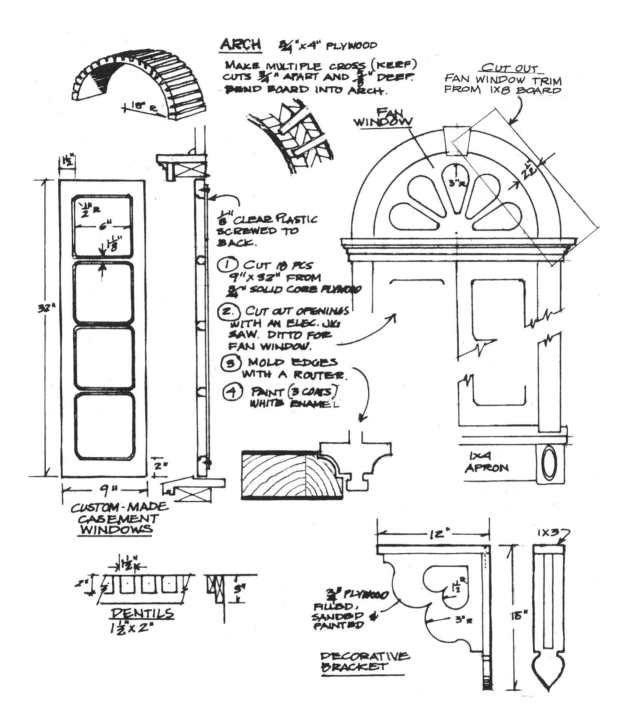

ARCH ¾"x4" PLYWOOD
MAKE MULTIPLE CROSS (KERF) CUTS ¾" APART AND ⅝" DEEP. BEND BOARD INTO ARCH.

18" R

CUT OUT FAN WINDOW TRIM FROM 1x8 BOARD

FAN WINDOW

3" R

2½"

1½"

½" R
6"
1⅛"

32"

⅛" CLEAR PLASTIC SCREWED TO BACK.

① CUT 18 PCS 9" x 33" FROM ¾" SOLID CORE PLYWOOD

② CUT OUT OPENINGS WITH AN ELEC. JIG SAW. DITTO FOR FAN WINDOW.

③ MOLD EDGES WITH A ROUTER.

④ PAINT (3 COATS) WHITE ENAMEL

2"

9"

CUSTOM-MADE CASEMENT WINDOWS

1x4 APRON

1½"
2"
3"

DENTILS
1½ x 2"

12"

1x3

1½" R

3" R

18"

¾" PLYWOOD FILLED, SANDED & PAINTED

DECORATIVE BRACKET

Figure 8.13—Victorian Shed window details

Figure 8.14—Pool Shed

Pool Shed

This luxurious and practical pool shed combines a dressing room, storage room, outdoor barbecue and wet bar (see Figures 8.14, 8.15). Smoke from the barbecue exits through the rear window and open cupola. If the weather becomes inclement, guests can move inside and sit around the circular table.

This shed makes a nice spring project. Depending on whether you devote yourself to this project part or full time, it should take between three and eight weeks to build. It requires advanced masonry and other construction skills and the ability to act as contractor to job out some of the tasks. Highlights of this shed's construction follow.

Level a 30 x 26-foot area on which to build. If you hire a backhoe operator, have him also dig your foundation trench (see Figure 8.16). Set offset stakes as described on pages 14-16, fill the excavation with 8

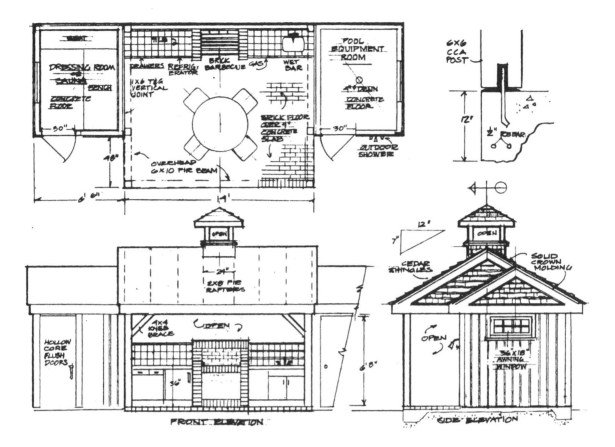

Figure 8.15—Pool Shed plan and elevation

inches of 1-inch-diameter gravel or crushed stone. Then have a concrete slab poured as described in Chapter 2, pages 17-19.

Build the shed using 6x6 pressure-treated posts, 4x4 pressure-treated knee braces, and 2x8 #2 construction fir rafters. The enclosed rooms are framed with 2x4s. All the posts are positioned to the slab by embedding ½ x 10-inch anchor bolts into the concrete while it is wet. To allow for misalignments, drill an oversize hole in the bottom of each post and fill it with auto-body putty. Before it has a chance to set, slip the post over the pin and align the post plumb.

Leave a 24x4-inch opening in the roof for the cupola and build it into the roof. Cover the roof with 1x4 spaced sheathing and 18-inch cedar shingles. Build the cupola using 4x4 cedar corner posts and allow for a 12-inch high opening for the smoke to get out. To protect the underneath part of the cupola roof from the occasional spark, cover it with galvanized sheet metal. Shingle the roof and install a (grounded, if metal) weather vane.

Custom design your interior with materials that stand up to any weather(see Figure 8.17). If you hook up a water supply from the house, make sure it is sloped down to a disconnect plug for drainage.

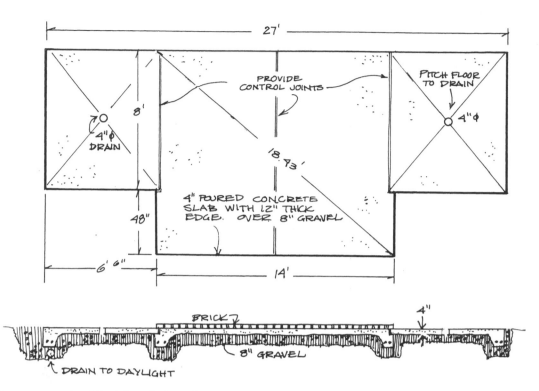

Figure 8.16—Pool Shed foundation plan

Figure 8.17—Pool Shed interior

Figure 8.18—Play Shed

Play Shed

In a child's mind, this shed can be a log cabin, a fort, a jungle gym, or a quiet place to spend some time reading a book. This 8x8-foot structure is built primarily out of cedar 4x4 posts and can be built in two days (see Figure 8.18).

Since most power circular saws cannot cut through a 4x4 in one pass, it's better to have your lumberyard cut the 4x4s on a large radial arm saw.

Number of 4x4s required:

    42 pieces 4 inches
    22 pieces 24 inches
    17 pieces 48 inches
     6 pieces 72 inches
    10 pieces 96 inches

Using two pieces of ¾-inch CDX plywood, build an 8x8-foot platform. Nail 2x4 CCA to the back and flip the platform over, right side up (see Figure 8.19).

Using a drill press and/or a portable electric drill, carefully drill a ⅜-inch hole through the end of each 4x4 and each square block, so the

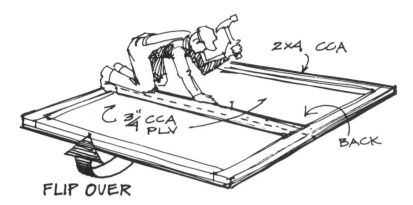

Figure 8.19—Play Shed roof

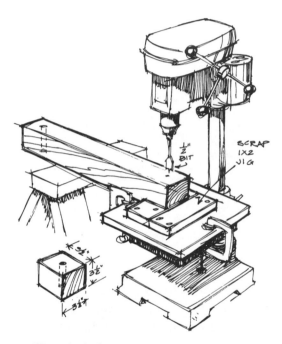

Figure 8.20—Drilling the holes

holes line up exactly on center. Build a jig (see Figure 8.20) to hold the 4 x 4s while you drill them.

Stack the pieces, Lincoln-log style, on a ⅜-inch reinforcing rod. As you proceed upwards, glue each piece with PL 40 adhesive (see Figure 8.21).

Build the roof using 2 x 4 rafters with 2 x 4 purlins notched into the middle of each rafter(see Figure 8.22). Make sure the notch for the purlins is on the top of the rafter, rather than the bottom. Assemble the rafters in pairs on the ground, and join them together at the top with collar ties made from scrap 2 x 4s. Leave a 1½-inch space between the top ends of the rafters for the 2 x 4 ridgepole. Tilt the rafters into place, slip the ridgepole and purlins into their respective notches, and nail them in place. Caulk and nail 1 x 10 #1 select cedar roof boards to the

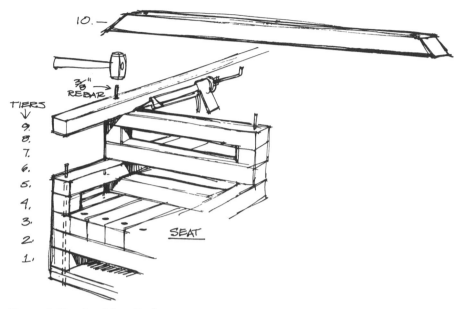

Figure 8.21—Stacking the logs

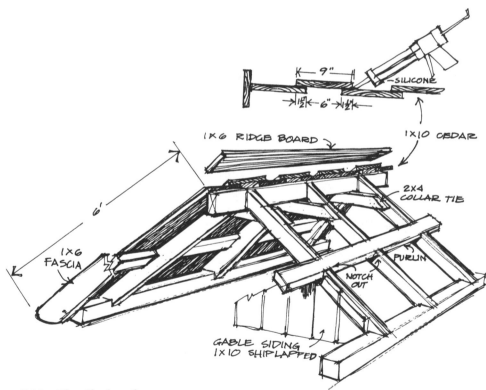

Figure 8.22—Play Shed roof

roof, overlapping them 1½ inches along the sides. Cut and fit four 1x6 fascia boards to the front and back gables, nailing them to the ends of the ridgepole, purlins and roof boards. Cap the roof by installing two 1x6 ridge boards.

Figure 8.23—Pavilion Shed

Pavilion Shed

This pavilion shed is a sheltered recreation area suitable for casual dining and entertaining (see Figures 8.23 and 8.24). Although it is shown here perched over the water (requiring expensive pile driving), it can be built more economically on land. Construction highlights follow.

The pavilion shed is is basically a 12 x 12-foot room, constructed outdoors on an elevated deck, and supported by 8 x 8-inch pressure-treated poles, sunk into the ground. Double doors open on each side, allowing

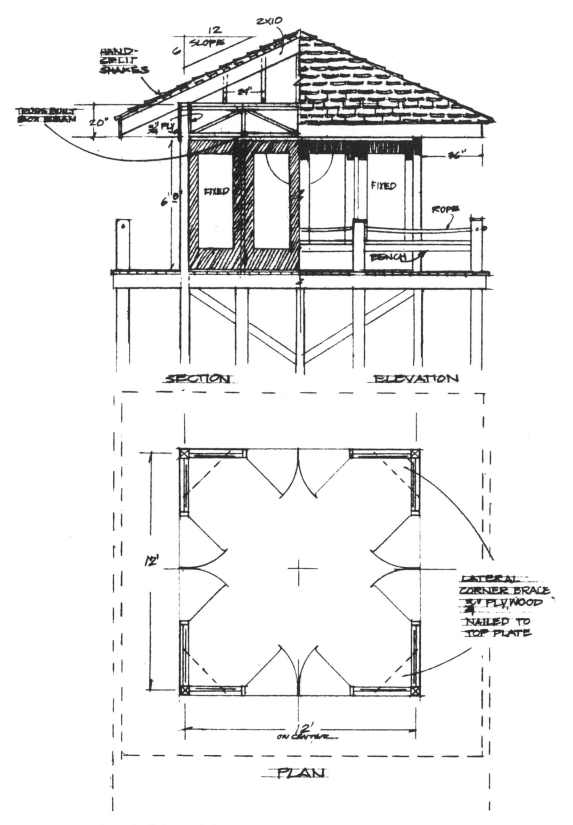

Figure 8.24—Pavilion Shed plan and elevation

maximum light and air circulation. The 16 doors are lightweight combination-doors with interchangeable screens and glass panels. Storage for the panels not in use can be built in under the floor. Note the use of diagonal support beams (see "triangulation," page 11) to protect the structure against wind load. To strengthen the shed even further, a truss-built, plywood box beam is securely joined to the four 6 x 6 corner posts (see Figure 8.25).

After marking the post placement, dig 21 post holes, 12 inches in diameter, 4 feet into the ground. You can use round posts, as shown in the sketch, but it is easier to use square, 6 x 6 pressure-treated lumber. Set the posts into their holes, but do not backfill until you have aligned the posts perfectly (see Japanese Boat Shed, page 99). Connect the posts with temporary braces and build the floor framing (see Figure 8.26).

Cover the floor framing with 2 x 6 tongue-and-groove decking, spanning a maximum of 6 feet between supports.

Build a truss box beam (see plans) over the doors. This connects the four corner posts of the room and provides a strong header for the roof. Frame the hip roof with 2 x 10 construction fir lumber, similar to that of the Japanese Boat Shed (see Figure 6.3).

From a sheet of ¾-inch plywood, cut four 2-foot triangles and nail them to the tops of the corners for additional strengthening.

Shingle the roof, using hand-split shakes, and nail a 1 x 10 fascia board to the tail end of the rafters.

Drill holes in the protruding perimeter, and run a 1½-inch nylon rope through the posts to act as a rail. Build a bench out of cedar 2 x 6s and ⁵⁄₄ x 6 boards. Install the doors so that they swing in, as shown in the plan. Stain the entire structure in a color of your choice and invite your friends over for a barbecue.

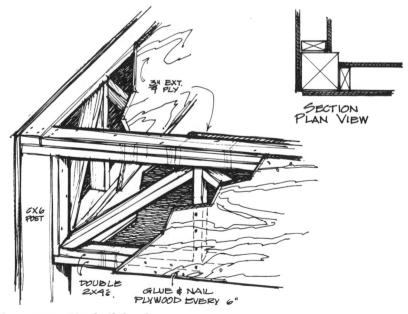

Figure 8.25—Site-built box beam

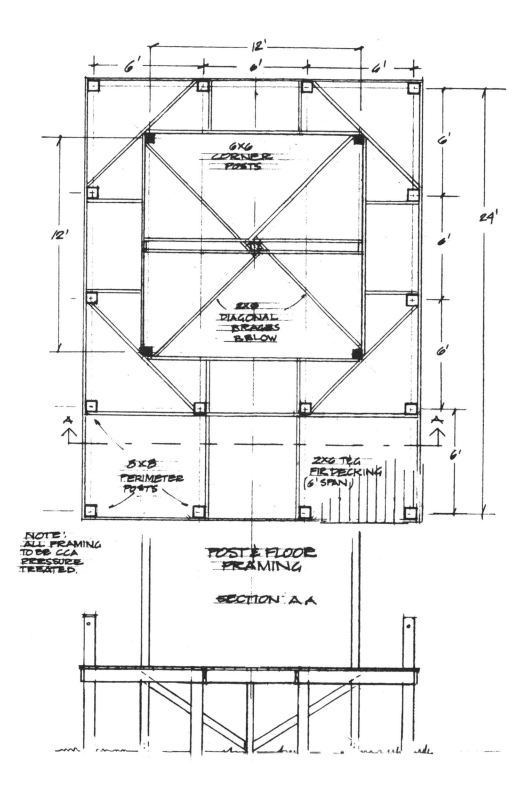

Figure 8.26—Pavilion Shed plan and elevation

Boat Shed

CHAPTER 9

Inspirations

✿

A private sauna, a silver cedar-shake boat shed with a panoramic ocean view, a country hideaway with a double Dutch door—you can turn contemplative visions into real places with willpower and hammer power.

Here is a collection from the whimsical (the oriental shed) to the practical (the attached garden shed) to the fantastic (the free-form ferro cement shed).

In the photograph section, the following sheds were designed by the author: Work Shed, Bike/Garden Shed, Firewood Shed, Irish Garden Shed, Basic 8 x 10 Shed, Pool Pavilion, Japanese Boat Shed, 9 x 10 Storage Shed on Posts, Three-Sided Tool Shed, 7 x 9 Shed/Play-house, Storage Shed with Three-Gable Roof, and 10 x 11 Potting Shed.

Oriental Shed

Tea Shed

Howard's End

Tudor Shed

Facing page:
Darcy's garden and wood shed
Sag Harbor, New York

Hamptons doghouse
East Hampton, New York

*The author's
work shed
East Hampton,
New York
(above)*

*Firewood shed
East Hampton,
New York
(right)*

Bike/garden shed,
East Hampton, New York (top)

Pool equipment shed (above) designed by Gary
Crain Assoc., New York, New York

Detail, Irish Garden Shed
East Hampton, New York (right)

Basic 8 x 10 Shed
Amagansett, New York (above)

Restored smokehouse
East Hampton, New York (right)

Folly-On-Wheels
Southampton, New York (below)

Birdhouse shed
Bridgehampton, New York (above)

Studio of E. H. Rubye Copus, wood sculptor
East Hampton, New York (right)

Eastland Farms nursery shed
Water Mill, New York (below)

Pool pavilion
Bridgehampton, New York, (above)

"Privy" shed
Sagaponack, New York (left)

Potting shed
Bridgehampton, New York (above)

Pool changing shed
Sagaponack, New York (right)

Meadow shed
Sagaponack, New York (below)

Simone's gazebo
East Hampton, New York,
(above)

Japanese Boat Shed
Sag Harbor, New York (right)

9 x 10 Storage Shed on Posts
(facing page), designed and built
by author. For instructions and
illustrations, see page 107.
Photograph by Jean Stiles.

Three-sided tool shed designed and built by author. New York City town house garden (right). Photograph by David Stiles.

7 x 9 shed/playhouse designed and built by author. East Hampton, New York (below). Photograph by David Stiles.

10 x 11 Potting Shed (above) designed and built by author. For instructions and illustrations, see page 119. Photograph by David Stiles.

Artist's studio with heat and electricity. Hampton, New York (right). Photograph by David Stiles.

Pool pavilion at dusk. East Hampton, New York (above). Photograph by Jean Stiles.

Storage shed with three-gabled roof and salvaged window, designed and built by author. East Hampton, New York (right). Photograph by David Stiles.

*Well shed (right).
Photograph
by Skip Hine.*

*Shed made from
an old chicken coop
(below). Photograph
by David Stiles.*

Milk shed (above). Photograph by David Stiles.

*David Hense's tea house shed
in Olympic, Washington (below).
Photograph by David Hense.*

*Artists Ann and John Hulsey's garden shed with
recycled windows and China at the entrance.
Lawrence, Kansas (above). Photograph
by John Hulsey.*

Thatched writer's retreat in secret garden (facing page). Photograph by Jean Stiles.

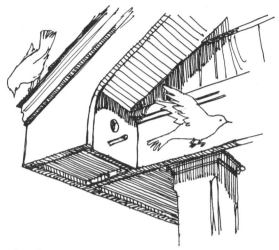

Cornice return

Birdhouse Shed

Bungalow

Gambrel-Roof Shed

Barn Shed

Shed with garbage addition

Curved-Roof Shed

Western Shed

Log Shed

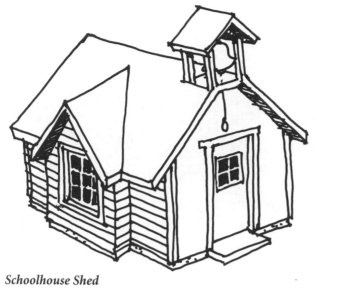

Schoolhouse Shed

Cross-Gable Shed

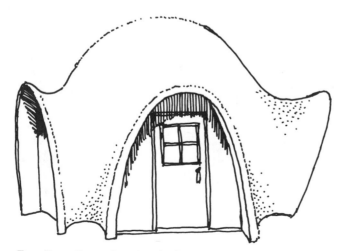

Free-Form Ferro Cement Shed

Play Shed

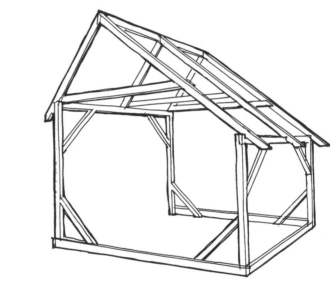

Saltbox frame

Pergola

Minaret

French Turret Shed

A-Frame

Spring Shed

Simple Garden-Tool Shed

My mother's Garden Shed

Glossary of Shed Terms

Batten: a strip of wood to cover a seam between boards or a board used to reinforce a door

Bird's mouth: a right-angle notch made in a rafter where the rafter meets the wall

Box beam: a beam fabricated out of dimensional lumber and plywood, generally glued and nailed

Casing: enclosing frame around a door or window

Cats, side-wall and end-wall: horizontal 2x4s (nailers) between studs; while they help brace the wall, their main purpose is to provide a nailer on which to mount a shelf

CCA: chromated copper arsenate, the chemical used in pressure-treated lumber to help it resist rot; CCA also refers to pressure-treated lumber itself

CDX: an economical, low-grade plywood

Clapboard: horizontal sheathing boards beveled with one edge thicker than the other; used as siding

Clerestory: upper part of the wall containing windows for lighting the center of the room

Collar tie: a horizontal member, usually a 2x4 or 2x6, connecting rafters opposite one another in a double-sided roof; the collar tie keeps the rafters from spreading and pushing the building out

Cupola: small, dome-like structure built on a roof

Drip cap: aluminum strip flashing that goes over windows and doors

Eaves cap: aluminum strip that protects the edge of the roof

Eaves: edges of a roof that usually project beyond the sides of the building

Expansion joint: a fiber strip separating large areas of poured concrete to control cracking

Fascia: horizontal trim piece nailed to the ends of the rafters, just below the edge of the roof

Fixed-sash window: window that doesn't move or open

Folly: a whimsical or extravagant structure

Froe: hand tool with the blade set at right angles from the handle; used to split cedar shakes

Gable, gabled end: triangular wall enclosed by the sloping ends of a roof

Gambrel: barn-type roof with two sloping sides on each of its two sides, the lower being steeper than the upper

Girder, center girder: a large, usually horizontal beam supporting the floor joists or the framework of a building

Glulams: manufactured plywood beams

Green lumber: unseasoned lumber (but not green in color)

Gypsum board (or sheetrock): 4-foot-wide sheets of plasterboard used as wall covering

Header (or lintel): the heavy beam placed across windows, doors or other openings to support the weight above

Homasote: trademark name for gray composition board

Joist: parallel beam that holds up the boards of a floor

Kerf: space left from a saw cut

Lap joint: joint made by lapping one part over another and fastening them

Ledger board: a beam attached to the studs to support the joists

Linear foot: a measurement of lumber one foot in length

Lookouts: short beams that support the overhang of the roof at the gable ends

Mortise and tenon: a method of joinery in which a mortise (a rectangular hole or recessed cut) receives a tenon (a protruding part cut to fit)

Muntins: strips supporting and/or separating the panes of window glass

Nominal size: size of lumber by which it is commonly known and sold (not the actual size)

Offset stakes: stakes placed outside the proposed shed location

On center: distance from the center of one piece to the center of the next; common on-center distances are 16 and 24 inches

Plates, top and bottom: horizontal pieces on the top and bottom of a wall to which the studs are nailed; the bottom plate is also called the "sole plate"

Portable electric jigsaw: a high-powered, electrical saw with a reciprocating blade, used for rough-cutting existing walls, roofs, floors, pipes, etc.

Post and beam: a framing system in which heavy vertical posts support heavy beams that, in turn, support floors and roofs

Post-and-skirt foundation: a foundation in which posts sunk into the ground support a "skirt" that serves to cover the foundation

Pressure-treated wood: Pressure-treated wood (PT), because of its rot-resistant qualities, is a practical solution for supporting posts and framing that comes in contact with the ground. Because most PT wood contains CCA (chromated copper arsenate), precautions should be taken when working with it. These include wearing a mask and gloves when sawing the wood and washing all exposed areas of your skin before eating or drinking. Sealing the ends of pressure-treated wood with a moisture repellent helps lock in toxic chemicals and prolongs the life of the wood. All sawing should take place outdoors with a plastic tarp underneath the wood so that the sawdust will not leach into the ground and can be easily disposed of. Never burn pressure-treated wood.

Purlins: horizontal roof beams supporting rafters of a roof

Rafter: a structural member that slopes from the ridge of a roof to the eaves and supports the roof

Rake end: the overhang at the gable end of a roof; rake board or rake fascia is the fascia nailed to the ends of the look-out rafters supporting the rake end

Rebar: steel reinforcing bar that is used to reinforce concrete

Ridgepole: the horizontal board at the ridge of a roof to which the rafters are connected

Romex: trademark name for plastic-covered electrical wire

Router: an electric tool used to cut grooves and shape lumber into various molding profiles

Scab lumber: board cut from the outside edge of the tree that has a rounded side

Screed: a straight 2x4 used to level wet concrete

Shiplapped: siding in which boards are rabbeted along the edge to make a flush joint

Slab foundation: poured concrete foundation and floor

Slope: slant or pitch of a roof expressed by the ratio of its height to its run

Soffit: horizontal underside of eave or cornice

Sole: the bottom plate of a framed wall; see Plates, top and bottom

Spackling compound: powdery substance mixed with water to form a paste used to cover holes, cracks and tape in gypsum board

Structolite: trademark name for lightweight gypsum interior stucco

Stud: lumber used for the vertical framing members of a wall

T-hinge: T-shaped door hinge

Timber frame: see Post and beam

Toenail: a nail driven through a vertical board at an angle to fasten it to a horizontal board on which it is based

Tongue-and-groove: joinery in which the tongue or tenon of one board fits into the groove of the other

Triangulation: in framing, the use of a diagonal piece to brace, strengthen and square a rectangle

---

Abbreviations

ø = diameter, also dia.
& = and
alum. = aluminum
CCA = chromated copper arsenate
CDX = plywood sheathing
dia. = diameter, also ø
elec. = electricity
ext. = exterior
galv. = galvanized

ftg. = footing
h.c. = hollow core (door)
int. = interior
o.c. = on center
PT = pressure-treated wood
reqd. = required
RO = rough opening
T&G = tongue and groove
typ. = typical
w/ = with

Further Reading

Koel, Leonard. *Leonard Koel's Carpentry*. Homewood, IL: American Technical Publishers, Inc., 1991.

McRaven, Charles. *Building with Stone*. Pownal, VT: Garden Way, 1989.

Philbin, Tom, and Ettlinger, Steve. *The Complete Illustrated Guide to Everything Sold in Hardware Stores*. New York, NY: Macmillan, 1988.

Roy, Robert L. *Underground Houses: How to Build a Low-Cost Home*. New York, NY: Sterling Publishing, 1981.

Seddon, Leigh W. *Practical Pole Building Construction*. Charlotte, VT: Williamson Publishing, 1985.

Stiles, David and Jeanie. *Rustic Retreats—A Build-It-Yourself Guide*. Pownal, VT: Storey Books, 1998.

Stiles, David and Jeanie. *Tree Houses You Can Actually Build*. Boston, MA: Houghton Mifflin Company, 1998.

Syvanen, Bob. *Carpentry: Some Tricks of the Trade*, Second Edition. Old Saybrook, CT: Globe Pequot Press, 1988.

Note to Readers

If you have built a shed that you are particularly proud of, we'd be happy to see a photograph of it. Please forward any photographs to David Stiles, c/o Firefly Books Ltd., 3680 Victoria Park Avenue, Willowdale, Ontario M2H 3K1.

Index